"Faithful, encouraging, convicting, needed. Sanchez's *Seven Dangers* is all this and more. He demonstrates how Jesus' words to these seven ancient churches are as relevant to our churches and our hearts as ever."

JONATHAN LEEMAN,
Editorial Director, 9Marks

"I've heard (and preached) many sermons on Revelation's "seven churches" but this book brought them alive to me in a new way with a rare combination of precise biblical exposition and precise practical application. It reminded me again of the abiding relevance and cultural timelessness of the Scriptures. May God use this book to awaken us to the fearful dangers inside as well as outside the church, but also point us to the Lord of the church as our only and all-sufficient hope for the future."

DAVID MURRAY,
Professor of Old Testament and Practical Theology,
Puritan Reformed Theological Seminary; and author of
Jesus on Every Page, Reset and *Exploring the Bible*

"Combining careful exposition and practical application out of an experienced pastor's heart, this challenging book brings the text alive with penetrating parallels to our contemporary context. Unsettling and liberating in equal measure, its message deserves to be read and pondered by every church leader and member. Above all, its central focus is consistently on the gospel and on the Lord Jesus Christ himself, the head of his church, who is the only answer to our current predicaments. I warmly commend it."

Former

"Every church in every age needs to hear the voice of Jesus speaking to it. In these seven letters in Revelation there is encouragement, challenge, rebuke, and exhortation—all from the lips of Jesus himself. Juan has done a great job of making the voice of our ascended Savior and Master clear, vibrant, and relevant for the age in which we live. May God give us ears to hear what the Spirit is saying to the church!"

ADRIAN REYNOLDS
Training Director, Fellowship of Independent Evangelical Churches

"Juan Sanchez makes wonderfully clear the call of Christ to the churches in Revelation, and he helps open our ears to hear that call in the church today. This book doesn't minimize Scripture's life-and-death warnings, and it keeps before us the amazing promises of Christ's presence and power. All this comes in the voice of a wise, experienced, Scripture-saturated pastor/preacher. I read his words with great thanksgiving for the gift of this strengthening exhortation to the church."

KATHLEEN NIELSON
Senior advisor and editor for The Gospel Coalition;
and author of *Women and God*

"A convicting, challenging, and comforting exposition of Christ's message to the seven churches in Revelation. Juan Sanchez combines careful exegesis with incisive pastoral application. The message given to the seven churches needs to be heard afresh today, and Sanchez's book reminds us why these words are so needed in our cultural moment."

THOMAS R. SCHREINER
James Buchanan Harrison Professor of New Testament Interpretation,
The Southern Baptist Theological Seminary

"In *Seven Dangers Facing Your Church*, Juan Sanchez is not afraid to confront us with uncomfortable truths from the lips of Jesus about what it means to be church. His commitment to understanding what Jesus was saying to the first readers, combined with stunning insights into how we do exactly the same, make this a challenging read. Juan then goes further— with the experience of a pastor and a heart to win people, not arguments—he takes us to the cross, he calls us to repent, he shows us how to change. Simple but profound, this book provides a great spiritual health check of the life of our church."

LINDA ALLCOCK
London Women's Convention

"In this book, Juan Sanchez opens the arsenal of the Spirit and uses the sword of the word of God to address the perennial concerns of the church. *Seven Dangers* is soul-searching and splicing and strengthening—I recommend reading it with a pen in your hand and some friends by your side."

GLORIA FURMAN
Author of *Missional Motherhood* and *Alive in Him*

"This is a timely book. Dr. Sanchez looks at Jesus' assessment of the seven churches in the book of Revelation with biblical understanding and insightful applications. He searches the Scriptures and brings them to us in a clear and an engaging way from beginning to end. If you want to understand the condition of those churches to which these letters were addressed, and the dangers every church has faced in the last two thousand years, this book is for you."

MIGUEL NÚÑEZ
Senior Pastor, International Baptist Church, Santo Domingo

"The threats faced by the seven churches in Revelation aren't very different from what our churches face today; the church has always existed in dangerous times. Jesus' words to those churches are as timely today as they were two thousand years ago, and Juan Sanchez helps unpack the various dangers our congregations face today. This is a great resource and I cannot recommend it enough!"

MATT CARTER
Pastor of Preaching and Vision, The Austin Stone Community Church

"Writing for both church leaders and members, Juan Sanchez provides a tonic for the soul. *Seven Dangers* is easy to read yet hard hitting, gracious but incisive. Through careful yet simple attention to the text, he prises open contemporary challenges and encouragements that remind us of Jesus' concern for his church—and the real dangers of forgetting or ignoring this."

CARL CHAMBERS
Park Hill Evangelical Church, Brighton; and Chair of Cuba para Cristo

"Juan Sanchez does 21st-century congregations a great service in giving us these expositions of the early chapters of Revelation. As he so ably shows, the letter of Jesus to the seven churches in Asia Minor is also a letter to the churches of the 21st century, with huge relevance to us in our different contexts and situations. We need these messages, as have Christians of every generation."

ANDY LINES
Mission Director, Crosslinks

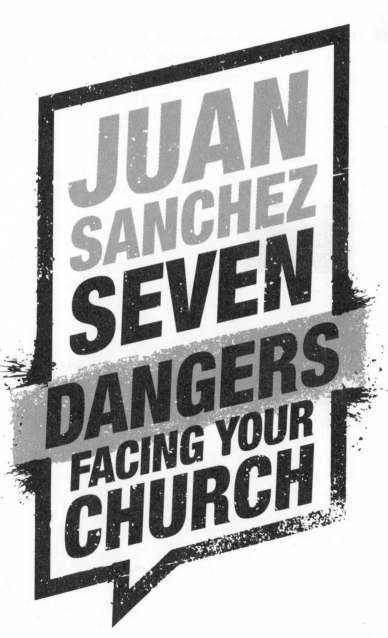

JUAN SANCHEZ

SEVEN DANGERS FACING YOUR CHURCH

To
First Baptist Church, Avon Park, Florida
Sunridge Baptist Church, Avon Park, Florida
Orange Heights Baptist Church, Hawthorne, Florida
First Baptist Church, Baldwin, Florida
First Baptist Church, Eastman, Georgia
Ryker's Ridge Baptist Church, Madison, Indiana
(Churches that cared for me and my family)

And to
High Pointe Baptist Church, Austin, Texas
(The church family I have the privilege to pastor)

Seven Dangers Facing Your Church
© Juan Sanchez/The Good Book Company 2018

Published by:
The Good Book Company
Tel (US): 866 244 2165
Tel (UK): 0333 123 0880
Email (US): info@thegoodbook.com
Email (UK): info@thegoodbook.co.uk

Websites:
North America: www.thegoodbook.com
UK: www.thegoodbook.co.uk
Australia: www.thegoodbook.com.au
New Zealand: www.thegoodbook.co.nz

ISBN: 9781784982782 | Printed in Denmark

Design by André Parker

CONTENTS

"*⁹ I, John, your brother and partner in the tribulation and the kingdom and the patient endurance that are in Jesus, was on the island called Patmos on account of the word of God and the testimony of Jesus. ¹⁰ I was in the Spirit on the Lord's day, and I heard behind me a loud voice like a trumpet ¹¹ saying, "Write what you see in a book and send it to the seven churches, to Ephesus and to Smyrna and to Pergamum and to Thyatira and to Sardis and to Philadelphia and to Laodicea."*

¹² Then I turned to see the voice that was speaking to me, and on turning I saw seven golden lampstands, ¹³ and in the midst of the lampstands one like a son of man, clothed with a long robe and with a golden sash around his chest. ¹⁴ The hairs of his head were white, like white wool, like snow. His eyes were like a flame of fire, ¹⁵ his feet were like burnished bronze, refined in a furnace, and his voice was like the roar of many waters. ¹⁶ In his right hand he held seven stars, from his mouth came a sharp two-edged sword, and his face was like the sun shining in full strength.

¹⁷ When I saw him, I fell at his feet as though dead. But he laid his right hand on me, saying, "Fear not, I am the first and the last, ¹⁸ and the living one. I died, and behold I am alive forevermore, and I have the keys of Death and Hades. ¹⁹ Write therefore the things that you have seen, those that are and those that are to take place after this."

Revelation 1 v 9-19

There's never been a more dangerous time for the church. It's swimming against the moral tide of culture, and is, frankly, struggling to keep its head above water.

From the outside, it faces growing oppression from tyrannical rulers and the reality of increasing persecution at the hands of an anti-Christian majority. From within, some church leaders are leading Christians astray with new and seemingly more attractive interpretations of Scripture. And those who are trying to stay faithful are left scratching their heads in bewilderment, at a loss over how to respond. The situation looks incredibly bleak.

But here's the thing: the church I've described in the paragraphs above is not, as you might have assumed, the church in the West today. It's a church in an entirely different time and place—Asia Minor in the 1st century—and the original recipients of the book of Revelation.

And this was a church in danger. They faced the pressures of living in a culture of rampant immorality and idolatry (referred to in Revelation as "the great prostitute"), the tyranny of an oppressive Roman regime ("the beast"), and discrimination from both the pagan Roman religious leaders and the Jewish synagogues ("the false prophet"), as well as the population at large ("those who dwell on the earth").

But behind the scenes, all these pressures were merely tools used by Satan ("the great dragon") in his attempt to destroy the church ("the bride of the Lamb").

Another church, two thousand years ago and several thousand miles away, and yet something in their experience rings true with our own today. And it's no surprise, because your church faces the same dangers at the hands of the same enemy, employing the same methods, using the same tools. Except that nowadays, that looks a little different. It looks like Christians being mocked on talk shows or sneered at on social media. It looks like Christians cowed into silence in their workplace because they fear losing their job. It looks like church leadership teams falling out over theological differences. It looks like denominations embracing a new definition of marriage. It looks like churches closing down and being snapped up by developers to be converted into something more "relevant." It looks like congregations losing heart because attendance is dwindling and the soul of their nation just seems so irreversibly lost.

There's no denying it. There's no point burying your head in the sand. Every church is in danger—and that includes yours. In fact, there are only really two kinds of churches: those who are soberly aware of the risks and are prepared to face them, and those who are carrying on completely unaware.

The devil is prowling on both. The question is: what are you going to do about it?

Dear Church, Love from Jesus

The good news is that Jesus *has done* something about the dangers facing your church—he wrote us a letter.

Most of us don't usually think of the book of Revelation as a letter, but that's what it is. It has a typical opening greeting and concluding blessing, and was written to and meant to circulate among seven churches in Asia Minor—what is now most of modern-day Turkey. Jesus wrote it in order to "show to his servants the things that must soon take place" (1 v 1). He intended to equip them to conquer these satanic threats to their faithful witness to Christ and his gospel. To deliver this message, Jesus chose the apostle John, their "brother and partner in the tribulation and the kingdom and the patient endurance that are in Jesus" (v 9). But this letter is unusual in that it is written in the genre of apocalyptic literature, which reveals both present and future events of judgment and salvation in vivid and memorable visions, dreams, images, and symbols.

John opens his message with a crystal clear promise: "Blessed is the one who reads aloud the words of this prophecy, and blessed are those who hear, and who keep what is written in it, for the time is near" (1 v 3). In other words, John fulfills the office of a prophet, and all who read, hear, and obey the words of this prophecy will be blessed; they will not be overcome by the dangers facing them. They will conquer; they will receive what God has promised; they will be blessed. And this promise is for you, too, and for your church.

So what exactly is it that we so badly need to hear? What is it that the church needs when it's distraught, weakened, threatened, and caused to wonder if God is in control? We need a vision. When there are many who are against us, we need a vision of the One who is *for us*: Jesus Christ. He's the One "who loves us and has freed us from our sins by his blood" (v 5-6). But he's not hanging on the cross anymore. In Revelation 1 v 12-20, John describes meeting Jesus face to face as he is now: risen, ascended, exalted, glorified. And there are three details which are particularly encouraging.

Jesus Is with Us

First, we see that Jesus is with us. As the apostle John is praying one Sunday, he hears a voice and turns around to see "seven golden lampstands, and in the midst of the lampstands one like a son of man" (v 12-13). A few verses later, Jesus explains that "the seven lampstands are the seven churches" (v 20). Revelation is written to seven specific churches in Asia Minor in the first century, but there were more than seven churches in that region at the time (see 1 Peter 1 v 1). The number seven, being a number of fullness, indicates that Revelation is written to all churches, including yours. "He who has an ear, let him hear what the Spirit says to the churches" (Revelation 2 v 7).

As a lampstand, each church is to hold up the light of the world: to be a faithful witness to Jesus and his gospel in a dark world. But notice the encouragement. Jesus, the Son of Man, is in the midst of his churches: ALL of them—the good ones and the bad ones (and we'll discover that there are plenty of the latter). In the face of danger, there is no greater promise that we or the first-century church could hear than this: that Jesus is present with us.

But Jesus is not just with us; he is with us to rule over us, protect us, and care for us and our messengers. "In his right hand" this shining figure holds "seven stars" (1 v 16). Jesus explains that the "seven stars are the angels of the seven churches" (v 20). Each church appears to have its own angel, who receives the message for each of the churches. What's important to note is that Jesus holds the "stars" in his right hand: the hand of power and authority, protection, and care. Jesus is sovereign over these messengers and, by extension, he rules over each of the angels' churches, caring for them and protecting them as a shepherd cares for and protects his sheep.

The dangers we face may feel overwhelming, but we will overcome them by looking to the all-glorious, risen Christ. He is with us; he cares for us; he protects us; he provides for us; he holds us in his right hand, from which nothing or no one can snatch us away.

Jesus Represents Us

Second, Jesus is our priest. John describes the figure in the midst of the lampstands as "one like a son of man" (1 v 13). This is the title Jesus often used of himself in the Gospels. It comes from Daniel 7 v 13-14, where Daniel witnessed "one like a son of man" receive a kingdom from the Ancient of Days. But the son of man is also dressed like a priest: he's wearing "a long robe" and "a golden sash around his chest" (Revelation 1 v 13), just as Israel's priests did in Exodus 28 v 4, 31.

Jesus is the One who finally and faithfully fulfills mankind's destiny to represent God to creation as a royal priest. This was the job given to Adam and Eve in the Garden of Eden: a job that they failed at miserably. But here we see Jesus doing it perfectly. As a priest, Jesus represents God before the world; he gives us a glimpse of what God is like. He reveals God's glory: "his feet were like burnished bronze, refined in a furnace" (Revelation 1 v 15), and "his face was like the sun shining in full strength" (v 16). He's the royal Son, who rules with divine wisdom, just like his Father: "The hairs of his head were white, like white wool, like snow" (v 14; Daniel 7 v 9). And because he is the royal Son, Jesus has received all authority to judge. Nothing gets past his gaze, for his "eyes were like a flame of fire" (Revelation 1 v 14). And he will judge swiftly, thoroughly, and fairly, for he will judge by the word of God: "from his mouth came a sharp two-edged sword" (v 16; 19 v 11-16).

As the wicked seem to continually prosper and have their way in the world and with the church, we can entrust ourselves to the just Judge. While the nations may rage against God's King, they won't be able to stand against his rule. But we don't need to fear Jesus' coming judgment, because we have entrusted ourselves to God's faithful Priest—one who not only represents God to us, but represents us before God. He himself became the once-for-all sacrifice for repentant sinners: he "freed us from our sins by his blood" (1 v 5). All who trust in Christ will not experience God's judgment, because Jesus has already received God's wrath in our place.

Jesus Speaks to Us

Finally, Jesus speaks God's words. Just as Israel heard the thunderous voice of God on Mount Sinai as "a very loud trumpet blast" (Exodus 19 v 16, 19), so too John hears Jesus speak in "a loud voice like a trumpet" (Revelation 1 v 10). Like Israel, John was overwhelmed when he heard Jesus' voice, for "his voice was like the roar of many waters" (v 15).

Jesus' voice is God's voice; Jesus' word is God's word. All who hear and read and keep his word will be blessed (v 3). This, surely, is a message worth listening to. In fact, the only appropriate response to this vision is to fall down before Jesus in fear and awe as John did (v 17). This Jesus is worthy of all our worship. We must bow down before him, and not before immoral culture, nor tyrannical governments, nor anti-Christian religions. The very dangers our church faces will either tempt us to deny Christ or move us to worship Christ.

And we worship him joyfully, not fearfully: "When I saw him, I fell at his feet as though dead. But he laid his right hand on me, saying, 'Fear not.'" What glorious words! Jesus is the all-glorious, risen King, but we, the church, are not to be afraid of him because Jesus is also our Savior, who "died, and … [is] alive forevermore" (v 18).

Where We're Heading

Following this stunning vision, in Revelation 2 and 3 Jesus goes on to expose seven dangers facing the churches in Asia Minor. Each message follows a similar pattern. First, he restates aspects of this vision that are relevant to each church as it faces its particular danger. Then, Jesus assesses each church, providing either commendation for what they're doing well or rebuke for where they're going wrong, or both. With the assessment, there is usually a call for repentance. But key to all the messages are the promises to overcomers which appear at the end of each message: promises that will be described in greater detail in Revelation 19 to 22.

Because Revelation is a circular letter, each church is to "hear what the Spirit says to the churches." Thus, the seven dangers are representative of dangers all churches have faced for the last 2000 years. So, over the next seven chapters, we'll unpack each message in turn. We'll look carefully at the text, and sketch in some helpful historical details. Then we'll explore what these same dangers look like in the life of your church today and, crucially, what to do to avoid them. Responsibility for guarding the church doesn't only lie with pastors and elders, but with every member too—so for that reason, this book is written for *everyone* who cares about their church.

A word of warning: this book will make uncomfortable reading in places. In fact, if it doesn't, it might be because you're not searching your heart hard enough. Most of us are good at seeing the dangers we're least at risk of and how they apply to others. Most of us are better at pointing the finger at our neighbor than we are at ourselves. So approach this book prayerfully, humbly, and thoughtfully—and keep your own church (as opposed to anybody else's) at the forefront of your mind.

And remember that Jesus does not merely expose these seven dangers and exhort us to overcome them in our own strength. Jesus calls us to live by faith in him and not by the sight of our circumstances. Revelation invites us to view this world, our church, and our lives from the perspective of God's throne room. Regardless of how bad things appear in this world, our sovereign God is on his throne (Revelation 4). And regardless of how out of control things appear in our lives, Jesus has received all authority in heaven and on earth and is carrying out God's eternal plan (Revelation 5). Jesus will vindicate his bride (Revelation 19); he will crush every enemy under his feet (Revelation 20); and he will lead us to our eternal inheritance (Revelation 21 – 22).

Forewarned by and forearmed with this prophecy, we can endure patiently in this world by faith in Christ. Be under no illusions: your church is in danger. But be in no doubt: you can overcome.

DANGER ONE
LOVELESS ORTHODOXY

[1] To the angel of the church in Ephesus write:

"The words of him who holds the seven stars in his right hand, who walks among the seven golden lampstands.

[2] "I know your works, your toil and your patient endurance, and how you cannot bear with those who are evil, but have tested those who call themselves apostles and are not, and found them to be false. [3] I know you are enduring patiently and bearing up for my name's sake, and you have not grown weary. [4] But I have this against you, that you have abandoned the love you had at first. [5] Remember therefore from where you have fallen; repent, and do the works you did at first. If not, I will come to you and remove your lampstand from its place, unless you repent. [6] Yet this you have: you hate the works of the Nicolaitans, which I also hate. [7] He who has an ear, let him hear what the Spirit says to the churches. To the one who conquers I will grant to eat of the tree of life, which is in the paradise of God."

Revelation 2 v 1-7

LOVELESS ORTHODOXY

I was fresh out of seminary. It was my first pastorate. What could go wrong?

After all, it's what I had trained for. All that Greek and Hebrew study, and surveys of the Old and New Testaments, not to mention dozens of classes on theology and pastoral ministry, were meant to prepare me to minister in the local church. And there I was. All I had to do now was faithfully preach God's word and the lost would come to know Christ, while believers would be built up in the faith. I felt confident that the church would naturally grow because, as I had read in some of those seminary books, "healthy things grow."

If only it were so simple. Looking back, I went into my first pastorate more concerned with making sure the church had all the "right" biblical doctrine and practices than I was concerned with caring for the spiritual health of the people who made up the church. Consequently, my sermons, while faithfully expositional, were too long. My patience for change, which the church needed, proved too short. On paper the church was moving in the right direction—but in reality, my heart was in the wrong place.

Whether they come from a seminary, a pastors' school, or a pastoral assistantship, most church leaders leave ministerial training with a head full of knowledge about right theology and right church practices. That's a good thing! But, if we're not careful, we can enter pastoral ministry more in love with the *idea* of a healthy church than with a true love for the church for which Christ died, and which is right in front of us. Too many of us enter ministry hoping to be the next John Stott or John Piper, or wanting to pastor the church of Mark Dever or Tim Keller. When we enter ministry with such theological and ecclesiastical idealism, the people we're called to shepherd will never measure up to our expectations. Instead of shepherding the flock of God that we are among, we end up shepherding the flock of God in our imagination. And in our imagination, we're always right; *they* (whoever "*they*" may be) are always wrong. When we get to that point in pastoral ministry, they always lose. But what we may not realize is, so do we. We lose credibility; we lose people's trust; and most dangerously, we may even lose the capacity to love Christ's sheep.

But the Christian in the pew is not exempt from the trap of ministry idealism either. You can probably think of some church members in your congregation who love theology (that person might even be you!); they love listening to the sermons of the celebrity pastors who are shaping contemporary evangelicalism. They read all the books, follow all the blogs, livestream all the conferences. And that's great too, isn't it? All God's people should love theology and grow from good preaching! But if that were me, rather than loving my church and my pastor, I'd be prone to develop an idea of what my church and my pastor should be like. If I were honest, I'd admit that I would rather be a member of St. Helen's Church, Bishopsgate or The Village Church, Dallas. I'd rather have Alistair Begg or John MacArthur as my pastor. And when that happens, I'm likely to develop a critical spirit. The preaching at *my* church will never be faithful enough; the theology at *my* church will never be right enough; and the practices of *my* church will never be biblical enough. When church members become so critical, *their* pastor can never win. But what they don't realize is, neither will they. Church members like these lose joy; they lose unity; and they too may lose the capacity to love the church family God has surrounded them with.

One caveat is necessary here: it is true that some pastors aren't faithful, and some churches aren't healthy. And as Christians, we're all called to "contend for the faith that was once for all delivered to the saints" (Jude 1 v 3). Sometimes this requires hard changes and difficult conversations. But throughout the New Testament, the plea to contend for the faith is matched by the command to love. We must never pit truth and love against one another.

I often think that it's reformed churches who are most at risk of focusing on truth at the expense of love, especially in our current cultural climate. As I travel throughout the United States and Latin America, I am both encouraged and humbled by the fresh awakening of Reformation theology I witness among young Christians. But at the same time, I am concerned by some of the extreme, unbiblical, and unloving applications of this theology being carried out by zealous, immature "reformers." It's no secret that the sea of cultural changes the church must navigate today requires us to stand for biblical faithfulness in a hostile world, and it's not uncommon for these cultural influences to invade and compromise the church. But because circumstances require that we contend for doctrinal purity, there's a danger that we emphasize right doctrine and practice to the neglect of love for others. In our rush to keep the church pure, we can forget to keep the church loving.

Yet this is not a new danger. In fact, it's the first danger the risen Christ exposes in Revelation 2 v 1-7: the danger of loveless orthodoxy.

Faithful under Fire

Before addressing the danger the Ephesian church faces, though, the risen Christ assures them of who he is. Jesus describes himself as the one "who holds the seven stars in his right hand, who walks among the seven golden lampstands" (2 v 1). John's already told us in Revelation 1 v 20 what the stars and the lampstands symbolize: "The seven stars are the angels of the seven churches, and the seven lampstands are the seven churches." And now we're told that Jesus "walks among" the lampstands (2 v 1). Notice both the authority and the love of Christ! Jesus "holds" their star; he has authority over their angel, and so the message that is about to follow comes with his supreme authority. But he also "walks among" his churches. He is with them. Before assessing the church and exposing their sin, he promises them his presence, care, and protection.

Christ's presence must have been especially reassuring for the Ephesian church, because first-century Ephesus was a hard place for gospel ministry. It served as a political, commercial, and religious center. Politically, it was the most important city in the Roman province of Asia. Commercially, it was a port city, facilitating trade and commerce. In terms of religion, it was home to one of the seven wonders of the world—the temple to the Greek fertility goddess, Artemis (Acts 19 v 23-34)—and also served as a center for the imperial cult, which honored Roman Emperors as deities. We can only begin to imagine the cultural pressures facing the Christians in Ephesus.

Sadly, we know from elsewhere in the New Testament that the church in Ephesus was not always healthy, and its pastors were not always faithful. In his farewell speech to the church's elders, the apostle Paul warned them that after his departure false teachers would emerge from among them "to draw away the disciples" (Acts 20 v 29-30). It seems that these concerns had materialized by the time Timothy assumed leadership at the church in Ephesus. Evidently, people with teaching authority had "wandered away" from sound doctrine (1 Timothy 1 v 3-7). Because elders possess the primary authority and responsibility to teach the church, and because Paul spends so much time in his first letter to Timothy addressing the qualifications of elders (3 v 1-7), it appears that the source of false teaching in Ephesus was their own elders, just as Paul had warned.

By the time Paul wrote his second letter to Timothy, the pressure for Timothy to compromise doctrinally and not preach the word was so great that Paul charged Timothy to preach the word, no matter how it might be received (2 Timothy 4 v 1-5), and to be willing to suffer for the sake of the gospel if required (1 v 8-14). Church leaders teaching false doctrine and church members refusing to tolerate sound doctrine are not the marks of a healthy church. No wonder Paul urged Timothy to "remain at Ephesus" (1 Timothy 1 v 3).

And yet, fastforward around 30 years to Jesus' words in Revelation, and it seems that the Ephesian church has managed to turn it around. They have labored to test and expose false apostles (Revelation 2 v 2); they have been "enduring patiently" in the face of pressure from outside and inside the church, for the glory of Christ's name; and in all this, they do not grow weary (v 3). Jesus recognizes that in this vibrant, cosmopolitan setting, the Ephesian church has not compromised their faith. Instead, they are persevering under all the political, cultural, and religious influences in the city, and toiling to maintain orthodoxy. They are working hard to maintain doctrinal purity, and Jesus commends that.

Perhaps you too know the pressures of living as a Christian in a cosmopolitan context. Cities such as London or New York, Shanghai or Dubai are in many ways not dissimilar to Ephesus—important centers of government, commerce, and even religion. Our cities now, as then, are hubs of diversity and often difficult ground for gospel ministry. Granted, Ephesus was under a totalitarian Roman ruler who could pressure the church in ways we Westerners may not yet experience today. But like the church in Ephesus, the church in the West today must maintain doctrinal purity in a hostile environment. We must not compromise!

And maybe you haven't—maybe you find yourself in a healthy church with faithful pastors. Your church preaches the gospel, loves sound doctrine, and reveres God's word. Your church courageously stands for truth and against cultural decay. If that's you, praise God!

But beware. Before you give yourself a pat on the back, know that Jesus' message comes with a sting in the tail. It's hard to imagine a more faithful church than the one in Ephesus. In a difficult ministry context, they crossed all their doctrinal t's and dotted all their ecclesiastical i's. Like you, they were doctrinally orthodox and theologically discerning. They didn't put up with traveling "gospel" salespeople who tried to introduce strange new teachings in the name of Christ. Their zeal showed no sign of waning.

But Jesus says, *That means nothing.* They lack one thing—and that one thing means everything. And we need to feel the force of the punch: that one thing is not sound doctrine.

The One Thing That Means Everything

"I have this against you," says the Lord Jesus to the church in Ephesus, "that you have abandoned the love you had at first" (v 4). To borrow from Paul, doctrinal purity without love is like "a noisy gong or a clanging cymbal." If we have right doctrine and right practices, "but have not love, [we are] nothing." If we discipline all false teachers and deliver all heretical curricula to be burned, "but have not love, [we] gain nothing" (1 Corinthians 13 v 1-3).

Sadly, this is precisely what the Ephesian church had done. They believed the right things and did the right things. They protected the church from evil people and false apostles. But for all their good, they abandoned love (Revelation 2 v 4). This is no minor offense. Remember that this is the first danger Jesus wishes to expose—out of seven churches, Jesus speaks to this one first. It's a danger that comes with a stark warning: unless they repent, Jesus will remove their lampstand (v 5). If they continue, they will forfeit their eternal claim on the very gospel they're so fiercely defending.

So this danger is serious. But what precisely does it mean to "abandon the love you had at first" (v 4)?

When Jesus was asked by a Pharisee, "Which is the great commandment in the Law?" he responded, "You shall love the Lord your God with all your heart and with all your soul and with all your mind." But Jesus continued, "And a second is like it: You shall love your neighbor as yourself. On these two commandments depend all the Law and the Prophets" (Matthew 22 v 36-40). Love for God is inseparable from love for others.

In his first letter, the apostle John also binds love for God and for others together, by arguing that our love for one another *flows out of* God's love for us. "Beloved," says John, "let us love one another, for love is from God, and whoever loves has been born of God and knows God" (1 John 4 v 7). In fact, "Anyone who does not love does not know God, because God is love" (v 8).

What is God's love like exactly? We see it most gloriously in his sending of Jesus to save us from judgment. "In this is love," explains John, "not that we have loved God but that he loved us and sent his Son to be the propitiation for our sins" (v 10). That simple verse should encourage your heart and assure your mind—if it doesn't, go back and read it again! Ponder it; savor it. This truth is personal, profound, and so simple all at the same time: "he loved us."

As we meditate on the truth of God's love for us in Christ, our hearts should be compelled in two directions. First, we should be moved to love and worship God. But for those of us who are theological consumers and zealous reformers, we must be careful that our love for God does not devolve into a mere love for theology. Once we've been gripped by God's grace, we naturally want to grow in our knowledge of God. But too often, this love for growing in *knowing God* becomes a mere love for growing in *knowing about God*. If we're not careful, God can become an impersonal subject of study. And when that happens, our heads will grow full with the study of doctrine, but our hearts will grow cold to the truth, beauty, and glory of the triune God. Every sermon we prepare, every Bible study we attend, and every podcast we listen to should lead us to a deeper love for God that moves us to respond in worship and praise and awe of him. That must always be the aim. If it's not, we're not just wasting our time; we're putting ourselves in danger.

Second, a deep love for others should flow out of our knowledge of God and his love for us. So, "anyone who does not love does not know God, because God is love" (v 8). Love is the undeniable mark of a Christian. Our love for one another not only informs the world that we follow Jesus (John 13 v 35), it also proves that Jesus is who he says he is (17 v 20-21). We're to be living evidence of the truth we proclaim. To abandon love (Revelation 2 v 3), is not, then, merely to lose your affection and zeal for the God who sent his Son to save us from his wrath—it is also a failure to love others.

It's not hard to abandon love. It doesn't happen all at once. Think of the new Christian. With great zeal, she devours the Bible and consumes two or three Christian books a week. But as her knowledge increases, so does her pride. Before she realizes it, she feels that she's grown past most Christians around her. Unlike her, she thinks to herself, they're lazy in Bible reading; unlike her, they're not serious about their sin; unlike her, they're too rooted in this world. As spiritual pride grows, our willingness to sinfully judge others increases. And as our willingness to sinfully judge others increases, our love for them grows colder and colder.

Or imagine a pastor who has grown weary with the Bible and God and his church, but then discovers Reformed theology. Never before has he been so in awe of God; never before has he been so aware of God's grace and sovereignty. For the first time in a long time, he's growing in his faith and in his love for God and Christ. But he quickly realizes that his congregation is not with him. His preaching has changed, they say. His sermons now seem harder to understand. They feel longer, in fact. And the pastor becomes defensive. He feels that the congregation is against him, but he commits to defending the true faith in spite of a cold reception. So he presses onward and forward. The sermons that once seemed hard to understand are now clear—clear in their condemnation, that is. They feel harsh to the congregation, but the pastor is convinced that he is faithfully separating the wheat from the chaff. Sadly, though, what he doesn't realize is that he has "abandoned the love [he] had at first."

Let's be honest. We all know that it's easy to lose love for those who criticize us, complain about us, or even attack us. It is in these contexts that Jesus commands us, "Love your enemies and pray for those who persecute you, so that you may be sons of your Father who is in heaven" (Matthew 5 v 44-45). But it's also easy to lose love for those whom we deem inferior to us in their doctrine and practices. Our unity and love for other believers is meant to be a powerful witness to the truth that the Father has sent his Son and that we are genuine Christians. That's why it grieves me to see brothers and sisters in Christ descend into heated arguments on Twitter or Facebook over minor matters of theology!

And let's remember that the hatred and vitriol hurled at us from a hostile, unbelieving world will only increase, but these people are not our enemies—they are our mission field. And those who are different than us but also follow Christ are not our enemies either—they are our family. We are called to love both. While there may come a time when we no longer associate with professing Christians who promote divisions and false teaching in the church (2 Timothy 3 v 1-9), the Bible nowhere grants us license to abandon love.

In his book *What Did You Expect?* Paul Tripp defines love this way: "Love is willing self-sacrifice for the good of another that does not require reciprocation or that the person being loved is deserving." I think that's a helpful definition of love. Because of God's love for us in Christ, and because of Christ's example of love for us, we are to live lives of willing self-sacrifice for others. The possibility that Jesus might remove the Ephesians' lampstand—and thereby remove their status as his church—shows us that it's possible to believe the right things and not be a church. It's possible to do all the right things and not be a church. It's possible to argue for the right moral values and not be a church. But if we practice genuine love for others, we will show the world that we are Jesus' followers, and that the Father has indeed sent his Son into the world to save the world.

Remember and Repent

Perhaps you're reading this and feeling increasingly uncomfortable—you can see that your love is growing cold. Take heart, there is good news.

When we recognize that we have neglected love, we must heed the risen Christ's warning to "remember ... from where you have fallen; repent, and do the works you did at first" (Revelation 2 v 5). In his mercy, Jesus shows us the way back. First, he tells us to "remember." Do you remember the freshness and vibrancy of your love for God and Christ when you first grasped the truth of the gospel? Do you remember how zealous you were for Christ, his word, and his church? Jesus calls us to remember how we used to love him.

Second, he calls us to "repent"—to turn away from lovelessness and to return to a love for others that flows out of our love for him. But in order to do that, we must change our thinking. That's what the word translated "repent" in verse 5 means. We need to replace the wrong ways of thinking with gospel ways of thinking. Perhaps, before you read any further, you need to put down this book, confess your lack of love to your Father, and ask him to fill you with a deeper knowledge of his love for you so that it flows out of your heart toward others.

And having changed our mindset toward God and the gospel and our opponents, we can, third, "do the works" of love that came so easily to us when we first came to faith in Christ.

How does that look on a whole-church level? First, pastors have a responsibility to model such love and help cultivate a culture of brotherly love within the church. And loving people starts with knowing people! One of the most useful tools we have at our church is a member directory with photos. We regularly encourage each member to pray through one page of the directory each day. We also ask them to use the directory to get to know other members they currently don't know. In addition, we urge our members to come to our services early and stay late just to have time to get to know and encourage one another.

There may be any number of ways that a church's leadership can encourage a loving culture: promoting hospitality, encouraging home groups, or fostering church-wide fellowship. But, most importantly, the leaders must model such love in their interactions with the church. So, when was the last time you had other members over for dinner? When was the last time you prayed for each member of your church by name? Do you know enough about what's going on in their lives to pray for their specific situations?

But Jesus' words in Revelation 2 v 6 remind us that the call to love is not a call to abandon truth. Jesus commends the Ephesian church because they "hate the works of the Nicolaitans, which I also hate." But notice what Jesus says. He commends the Ephesians, not for hating the Nicolaitans, but for hating their works. We don't know much about the Nicolaitans, but we'll come back to them in chapter 3. For now, we know all we need to know. Just as our works of love expose our love for God, so the works of the Nicolaitans expose their false doctrine. So, Jesus declares that he too hates the works of the Nicolaitans. He hates what they are teaching and the resulting works which that teaching produces.

When correction is required, however, those of us who are pastors must correct opponents in the church with kindness, gentleness, compassion, and love, praying that "God may perhaps grant them repentance leading to a knowledge of the truth, and [that] they may come to their senses and escape from the snare of the devil" (2 Timothy 2 v 25-26). When we model such compassionate correction for the sake of "our opponents," we are teaching our people how to address conflict in godly ways.

Not too long ago, our elders were made aware of a member who was promoting a false interpretation of a particular Bible passage on Facebook. It was oddly uncharacteristic of this member, but rather than bring down the hammer, one of our pastors reached out to another member who knows him well and whom this brother respects. The member finally emailed me, personally showing me the "evidence" for his interpretation. I responded by asking him a number of questions, and then laying out the case for a proper interpretation of the passage in question. It took some time, and I am not certain we fully convinced him, but he finally conceded, because he was standing alone in his interpretation against all these other brothers who love him and whom he respects. Admittedly, these conflicts don't always turn out well. But, if we're not loving, we won't be drawing people back to Christ and the church. We'll be driving them farther away.

Truth is important, but it cannot be separated from love. Love is important, but it cannot be separated from truth.

Paradise Promised

To those who do hold on to truth and love, Jesus goes on to make a wonderful promise: "To the one who conquers I will grant to eat of the tree of life, which is in the paradise of God" (Revelation 2 v 7). In paradise, God walked in the midst of his people in the garden in sweet, loving fellowship (Genesis 3 v 8). That the tree of life was in the garden meant this communion between God and humanity was to last forever. But when his people sinned, God removed them from his presence. Adam and Eve—and every human since—no longer had access to the tree of life. But here Jesus promises to open up access again. The Ephesian church, and your church, can come and eat and enjoy eternal life in God's presence.

The One who speaks to the Ephesian believers is none other than the One who walks among the churches (Revelation 2 v 1). If they do not repent, Jesus will remove their lampstand. They will no longer be a church; Jesus will no longer walk among them (v 5). But the one who conquers has nothing to fear. God will grant them access to the tree of life in the paradise of God, where God and his people will walk in perfect fellowship once again, but this time, for all eternity.

I've been involved in local church ministry since I was 19 years old, filling various roles on church staffs. But it wasn't until the fall of 2000 that I became a senior pastor for the first time. Within six months, the honeymoon period was already over. While my seminary studies had helped to lay a foundation for how to handle Scripture and think biblically about the church, nothing prepared me for the responsibilities of being the lone pastor of a congregation. Some of my resolutions were noble: I was determined to preach expositionally through whole books of the Bible; I decided not to implement any significant changes for the first year; and I hoped to help build up the church and remain their pastor for the rest of my ministry.

When I look back, though, I wonder if I was more in love with the idea of a healthy church than in love with the church as they were. Truth be told, it was the hardest season of ministry for me and my family. By God's grace we saw fruitfulness in ministry, but naïveté and immaturity abounded in both the pastor and the congregation. As hard as that ministry was, though, the Lord taught me that right doctrine and right church practices, while important, do not in and of themselves make a church a healthy community, or a faithful witness to the surrounding area.

Right doctrine is not sufficient—because love is essential.

DANGER TWO
FEAR OF SUFFERING

8 And to the angel of the church in Smyrna write: "The words of the first and the last, who died and came to life.

9 "I know your tribulation and your poverty (but you are rich) and the slander of those who say that they are Jews and are not, but are a synagogue of Satan. 10 Do not fear what you are about to suffer. Behold, the devil is about to throw some of you into prison, that you may be tested, and for ten days you will have tribulation. Be faithful unto death, and I will give you the crown of life. 11 He who has an ear, let him hear what the Spirit says to the churches. The one who conquers will not be hurt by the second death."

Revelation 2 v 8-11

FEAR OF SUFFERING

My parents couldn't afford to send me to university, so, to pay for my school, I enlisted in the United States Navy. In God's kindness, I eventually won a Navy scholarship to the University of Florida.

As a part of my training, I served on a tugboat one summer. Our job was to guide large ships through the harbor without incident, using only thick, heavy lines (ropes, to the non-nautical). One morning, the petty officer assigned to the tug was preparing the lines. You can imagine how thick and heavy they had to be to pull such large vessels, yet he was throwing them around like they were dental floss. As he organized the lines, he started to bad-mouth Christians, going on and on about how hypocritical and unreliable they were. Then he looked up at me, 19 years old at the time and only a Christian for two years, and he said, "You're not one of those Christians, are you?!"

That was it. That was the first moment of truth in my young Christian life. It was the moment to stand for my faith and muster the courage required not to deny my Lord. It was the moment to declare my allegiance to King Jesus and, in love, explain the gospel to this skeptic.

So, I responded, "Me? No, not me! I'm not one of those Christians."

Immediately, I was overwhelmed with grief; I felt physically sick in my stomach, and I remembered the disciple Peter who denied Jesus three times. But neither my grief, my ill-feeling, nor remembering Peter moved me to speak up.

What happened? Why, at that moment, did I become a coward? It's simple, really: I was afraid. I was afraid of what that intimidating, unbelieving sailor would think of me, what he might say to me, or what he could do to me. I was afraid to suffer, even if only a little, for the name of Christ. I suspect I'm not the only one.

Sooner or later, we will all be confronted with the choice of identifying with Christ publicly or denying him. It may be a young woman who comes to faith in Christ out of a Muslim background, and is afraid of her father and brothers. Or a husband from a Jewish background, who comes to faith in Christ and is forced to deal with the sense of betrayal felt by his parents and wife. Or a university professor from an atheistic background, whose entire career is in danger because of his newfound worldview. In all these circumstances, these new Christians will face suffering—owning their faith will potentially lead them to lose their life, their family, or their job.

But maybe that's not you. After all, not all suffering is life-threatening or career-ending, is it? Almost all of us will suffer social rejection, criticism, or ridicule for identifying with Christ. The friendship that goes cold; the snide remarks over the dinner table; the whispered gossip behind our back. These are small sufferings compared to some, but they still hurt. And they still force us to make a choice: will we identify with Christ or deny him?

Of course, not all denials of Christ look the same either. Some denials are public, verbal, and outright; others are "functional denials" by virtue of our silence. When we go about our lives trying to hide the fact that we belong to Jesus, we are denying Christ. When anti-Christian voices speak up against Jesus at school or work or our child's play group, and we remain silent while Jesus is decried and defamed, we are denying Christ. Consciously or not, we pursue the path of least resistance. We make sure not to draw too much attention to ourselves because of Christ. We keep our faith "private." We never say outright, "I don't belong to Jesus," but our silence screams it for us.

Yet so often in our churches, we either tacitly excuse or even promote this "heads down" mentality. We nod and smile and say, "Yes, that's hard," without ever challenging it or showing a better way.

Whether functional or actual, denial is denial. And such denials are almost always rooted in fear of suffering—even if the suffering is sometimes bigger in our imaginations than it would be in reality.

This is the second danger your church faces—that in the face of persecution, we would allow the fear of suffering to lead us to deny Christ. In the face of such a danger, Jesus exhorts the church not to be afraid of Christian suffering, but, instead, to remain faithful, even to the point of death.

But is he being wildly unrealistic? How can cowards like me overcome such fear? Jesus' message to the church in Smyrna shows us.

Making History

Located just north of Ephesus on the coast of the Aegean Sea, Smyrna (modern-day Izmir, Turkey) was the next city that was to receive the letter of Revelation. As with the messages to each of the churches, Jesus begins his message to the Smyrnan Christians by describing himself as exactly what they need. When we're afraid of what people may do to us, we need to remember that Jesus is "the first and the last" (Revelation 2 v 8). Jesus is the living, divine Word, who set history in motion by creating all things (John 1 v 1-3), and he is the Faithful and True Word of God, who will draw human history to a close when he returns to judge the living and the dead and establish the new creation (Revelation 19 v 11, 13). That's why Jesus can say of himself what can only be said of God: "I am the Alpha and the Omega, the first and the last, the beginning and the end" (22 v 13). Regardless of our circumstances—past, present, or future—Jesus controls history from beginning to end. He is Lord over all history, including the history we may not like.

But Jesus not only rules history; he entered history. He tells the Smyrnan church that he is the one who "died and came to life" (2 v 8). At a point in time some 2000 years ago, the ruler of history took on our humanity, lived, died, and rose again on the third day. Jesus' resurrection proves his victory over sin and death. And if we identify with this risen Christ, then we have confidence that even though we die, like him we will live again. As Christians, we may face great misery and terrible suffering at the hands of God's enemies. And we must face the reality that they may even take our lives. But whatever they may do to us, no human being can take our eternal life away.

Admittedly, though, when suffering does come, it still tends to surprise us, and simply knowing that we will rise again one day does not make suffering now feel easy. That's why Jesus has more to say.

The Shock of Suffering

The church in Smyrna needed to be reminded that Jesus was sovereign over history because, judging from their experience, he did not appear to be ruling over their present circumstances. They were facing "tribulation," "poverty," and "slander" (v 9). Smyrna was famous for its temple to the goddess Roma and became a center for emperor worship. Naturally, faithful Christians in Smyrna would have experienced social and political pressures to participate in idolatry and emperor worship. But the tribulation, poverty, and slander they faced likely arose primarily at the hands of the Jews in the local synagogue. Judaism was the only non-Roman religion permitted by law. Initially, Christians would have been considered a sect within Judaism, and granted legal protection to practice their faith. Over time, though, the Jews distinguished themselves from the Christian "sect," even handing them over to the governing authorities as those who refused to worship Romans gods and recognize Caesar as lord.

Jewish opposition to Christianity was nothing new—episodes from the book of Acts help us to imagine what this might have been like for the Smyrnan Christians. In Antioch of Pisidia, also in Asia Minor, Paul explained the gospel in the synagogue to a great reception (Acts 13 v 14-43). But on the next Sabbath, when large crowds came to hear Paul preach "the word of the Lord," the Jews "were filled with jealousy and began to contradict what was spoken by Paul, reviling him" (v 45). Though the gospel flourished, "the Jews incited the devout women of high standing and the leading men of the city, stirred up persecution against Paul and Barnabas, and drove them out of their district" (v 50). Something similar happened in Iconium, where "an attempt was made by both Gentiles and Jews, with their rulers, to mistreat them and to stone them" (14 v 5). Paul and his companions fled to Lystra, but "Jews came from Antioch and Iconium, and having persuaded the crowds, they stoned Paul and dragged him out of the city, supposing that he was dead" (v 19).

Why such fierce opposition? The Jews were jealous because they considered themselves, not these Gentile Christians, to be the true people of God. It was *they* who were awaiting their Messiah to return and restore Israel. But Christians were announcing that Messiah had already come and was already restoring God's people through the new covenant inaugurated by Jesus' death and resurrection. Ironically, by opposing the Christians in Smyrna, the Jews were actually opposing their Messiah and proving that they were, in fact, not true Jews—not the true people of God. Instead, they were children of Satan because, like their father, they opposed Christ and the true people of God: those who embraced Jesus, the Jewish Messiah.

Satan is a liar and a murderer. He is opposed to Christ. In Revelation 12, John will see that Satan, the great dragon, sought to murder Jesus (12 v 1-6), but Jesus defeated Satan through his victorious death and resurrection (v 7-12). When

Satan realized his defeat, he began making war against the church (v 13-17). It's for this reason that Jesus calls the Jewish synagogue in Smyrna "a synagogue of Satan" (2 v 9). These are shocking words, but no more shocking than Jesus speaking to Peter as "Satan" for attempting to hinder him from fulfilling his mission to die on the cross (Matthew 16 v 23-24). Satan is behind all opposition to Christ—whether that opposition comes from a disciple, from ethnic Jews, or even from us (Ephesians 4 v 27). Satan failed to defeat Jesus; now he is after the church.

The Jews in Smyrna were likely handing the Christians over to the Roman authorities for their refusal to acknowledge Caesar as Lord. When Jesus speaks of the "slander" of Christians by the Jews in Revelation 2 v 9, the word translated "slander" is literally "blasphemy." In other words, while the Jews were slandering Christians before the Roman authorities, they were, in actuality, practicing blasphemy against God. As a result of Jewish slander, the Smyrnan Christians experienced both physical suffering and economic oppression. We're told later in Revelation that those who refuse to bow down to the beast (the emperor and his government) will be unable to "buy or sell unless [they have] the mark, that is, the name of the beast or the number of its name" (13 v 17).

Like the church in Smyrna, many of our brothers and sisters in Christ throughout the world face religious opposition today. In Iraq, for example, the Islamic State in Iraq and Syria (ISIS) have led a sustained campaign to extinguish Christianity. Iraqi Christians have been forced to flee their homelands, experiencing tribulation, poverty, and slander. Religious oppression at the hands of Islamic extremists is rampant, not only in the Middle East, but also in parts of

Africa, Asia, and even Europe. And yet many of our brothers and sisters remain steadfast. The church in the West must make sure they do not suffer alone. We must, instead, weep with those who weep, pray for them, and do what we can to support them practically and financially.

In the West, we don't necessarily face such heated religious oppression, because Christianity has enjoyed majority status within our culture. On one level, this message to the church in Smyrna should serve as a warning to us not to use our privileged status against religious minorities. We should stand for religious freedom for all, because the day we permit religious oppression against one group, we open the door for religious oppression against every group.

Great Expectations

But this message in Revelation warns us against fear of all kinds of suffering for the name of Christ. It may be subtle, but this fear operates on both a conscious and subconscious level.

Consciously, this fear may stop us from even considering serving in a difficult mission field. Is it possible that we have so idolized Western comfort and security that we would object to our own children and grandchildren serving in dangerous contexts: say, in parts of the world where our Christian brothers and sisters are already suffering? In such cases, we may mask our fears behind a façade of wisdom as we seek to protect our family from potential dangers—but it is fear, nonetheless.

Subconsciously, the idea of comfort and security as a right is so ingrained in our Western psyche that, deep down, most of us expect to serve the Lord at no personal cost at all. And if left to our own devices, that's what we'll do. While the

Smyrnan believers faced "tribulation," we expect peace. While they experienced "poverty," we expect prosperity. While they endured "slander," we expect honor. We encourage our kids to study hard at school so that they can grow up to enjoy a life of peace, prosperity, and honor too. And when our expectations are not met, we assume that something has gone wrong. If we're honest, at times following Jesus doesn't seem worth it.

This subconscious fear of losing our comfort shapes so many of our choices. Rather than pursue ministry where Christianity is a minority religion and Christians are persecuted, we may, instead, pursue ministry in contexts that indulge our personal comforts and preferences. Rather than living in a run-down neighborhood where there aren't many Christians, we attempt to have our cake and eat it as we serve Christ while living in our upper middle-class home and driving around town in our luxury car. And rather than being willing to minister where we are unwelcome and unwanted, we minister to people who like us because we are just like them. We don't want to suffer; we want to be comfortable. But this message warns us that such expectations for the Christian life are woefully misguided.

Don't get me wrong. There is great need for gospel ministry in the West. I live in the United States in Austin, Texas, where by many reports, over 80% of the population is unchurched. With over 150 people moving into metro Austin each day, we can't plant churches fast enough just to keep up with the population growth. Gospel ministry is hard here, but for different reasons. And yet, Austin is also a great place to live. It's young; it's fitness conscious; it's progressive; it's beautiful; it's artsy; and it's got everything any vibrant, creative young adult would want, including great food and music. It's no surprise that Austin is a church-planter's dream. But I'm curious how many of the seminary graduates and church-planters who come here do so more out of a love for what the city offers them than out of a love for the unbelieving peoples in town. I'm all for becoming "all things to all people, that by all means [we] might save some" (1 Corinthians 9 v 22), but when contextualization becomes more about brewing your own beer, smoking the best cigars, and getting culturally appropriate tattoos, I have to wonder if such "contextualization" is about winning unbelievers to Christ or simply about indulging our personal preferences.

Now, I'm not against beer, cigars, and tattoos. Christians are free to enjoy them, so long as they practice such freedoms in love for their weaker brothers who choose to abstain. My point is simply that *we do not naturally gravitate toward danger*. Let's face it—brewing beer, smoking cigars, and getting tattoos is not dangerous ministry; it's just doing what most other hip people are doing.

When deep down we're afraid to suffer for our faith, we will gravitate away from suffering and toward comfort, security, and privilege. This happens on an individual level, and on a whole-church level too. Think of the small, middle-class church that's located in a transitioning neighborhood. As people from a lower socio-economic class move in, property values plummet, crime increases, and ethnic diversity grows. But rather than staying in the neighborhood to reach this new mission field, the congregation decides to sell their property to developers in order to move to the white, middle-class suburbs. Or imagine a church that's struggling to grow because it just doesn't have a culture of evangelism. The membership is faithful, but static. Christians are reluctant to engage in personal evangelism because they're afraid of the reception they'll receive. Or imagine a drug addict who starts turning up at Sunday services and is met with little else but a cold shoulder, because members are reluctant to get involved with someone so "messy."

It's imperative that pastors (elders) and church leaders equip their churches to endure suffering and hardship, and even embrace it. If we don't, members will always choose comfort over risk. When pressure comes from friends and family, they'll be tempted to deny their Savior. And worse still, if they are taken by surprise when the hard times come, they may decide that following Christ just isn't worth it.

So how do we protect ourselves and our churches from the threat of fear?

Get Ready

First, we must prepare for Christian suffering. Notice how Jesus does that for the church in Smyrna. He explains the reality of suffering—he tells them they "are about to suffer"—but he commands them not to be afraid (Revelation 2 v 10). In the West today, most Christians are not persecuted—not really, not yet. But nonetheless, as we read our newspapers or watch our news shows, we're convinced the world is unravelling. We complain about unbelievers acting like, well, unbelievers. And we fear we'll get caught up in the "tribulation," "poverty," and "slander" meant for us by the anti-Christian populations. But Jesus shows us how to read the news with faith, not fear. In fact, he tells us there is no need to be afraid.

While we may follow Christ into suffering or even death, we do not need to be afraid because our present suffering is only slight and momentary compared to the eternal weight of glory that awaits all who conquer their fears (2 Corinthians 4 v 17). Jesus reminds the church in Smyrna that their suffering is temporary; he tells them that they will suffer imprisonment for only ten days (Revelation 2 v 10). Regardless of how you interpret the numbers in Revelation, Jesus' point is that their suffering will be limited. While our suffering may not end in this lifetime, it still pales in comparison with the eternity of joy that lies ahead. Understanding the reality of suffering and its limits will help us endure faithfully.

Second, Jesus reminds the Smyrnan Christians that the real source of their suffering is Satan himself. The Jews in Smyrna were a synagogue of Satan because, like Satan, they opposed Christ and his church, the true people of God. After Satan lost the war against Jesus, he began to make war against us, Christ's church (12 v 13-17).

Remember Christian, our battle is not against other people—not even our persecutors; our battle is against Satan and his demons. Our battle is a spiritual battle. As we saw in the last chapter, unbelievers in this world who stand against us are not our enemies; they are our mission field. We must love those we are prone to think of as "enemies" and pray for those who persecute us—pleading that through our faithful witness, they too may come to know Christ.

Finally, Jesus tells the church in Smyrna the reason for Christian suffering—"that you may be tested" (2 v 10). On the face of it, it may not be very comforting to hear that our Lord permits us to suffer in order to test our faith. But if we stop and think about it—if we understand what Jesus is saying— we will realize that all Christian suffering is purposeful. Our suffering, both as individual Christians and as churches, is a means by which our Father in heaven is conforming us to be more and more like Jesus (Romans 8 v 28-30). When our faith holds up under the weight of suffering, it proves it is genuine, and this in turn increases our confidence. Even if all our worst fears become reality, God will use it for our good. It's not always obvious how—indeed, suffering may leave us feeling spiritually bruised and brittle, perhaps even for a very long time. But even then, we can hold on to this promise that our pain will not go to waste.

I had the privilege once of hearing Helen Roseveare speak. With a doctorate in medicine from Cambridge University in England, Helen could have practiced medicine in the comfort and security of Great Britain. Instead, as a young Christian, she gave her life to serve Christ as a missionary doctor in the Belgian Congo (later Zaire, now DRC). After civil war broke out in 1964, Helen, along with a few other missionaries, was placed under house arrest. In October of that same year, she was brutally raped. After initially questioning God's care for her during that time of suffering, she eventually "sensed the Lord saying to her…"

> *You asked me, when you were first converted, for the privilege of being a missionary. This is it. Don't you want it? … These are not your sufferings. They're mine. All I ask of you is the loan of your body.*

The day I heard Helen Roseveare share her life story, I did not see a woman who was afraid of suffering for Christ. I saw a woman who had conquered her fear, knowing that what she faced wasn't even her own suffering. It was the suffering of her Lord, and she counted it a privilege to share in it.

I have to confess that as a father of five daughters, it's still hard for me to recall Helen's story. Even as I write these words, I am convicted by her faith and moved to tears by her experience. Although she died in 2016, Helen's life still teaches us that Jesus does not waste our suffering; he purposes our suffering to strengthen our faith as a means for our perseverance (1 Peter 1 v 6-7). I know it may be hard to understand, but God permits Christian suffering for his glory and our good: that we would be conformed to the image of Christ.

So let me ask you: do you believe that? And if you do, will you let this truth strengthen your heart so that it may overrule the fear that so often lurks in your head? Think back over some recent decisions you've made—as an individual or as a church. Is it possible that you were motivated by fear, consciously or subconsciously? If so, will you revisit those decisions?

What about your church family? Are they under the impression that the Christian life is ultimately comfortable? Are these things being addressed from the pulpit? Do you chat about them over coffee? Do you challenge these expectations, or do you excuse them with a polite smile or your silence? If we don't do these things, then we are leaving our brothers and sisters exposed, because fear is very powerful—but Christ is more powerful still.

Bring It On!

As we grow in our understanding of Christian suffering— its reality, its source, and its purpose—we will be able, by faith, to heed the Lord's command to "be faithful unto death," because this command comes with a promise to all who endure faithfully: "… and I will give you the crown of life" (Revelation 2 v 10). Here, eternal life is pictured as "the crown of life"—a crown given to victors. To the victor go the spoils—and this is a prize of inexpressible value.

As we follow Jesus, we don't just follow him into suffering and death; we also follow him into resurrection and glory, for he is the one "who died and came to life" (v 8). Jesus says that all who conquer the fear of suffering and death by faith in him, and who endure faithfully to the end, "will not be hurt by the second death" (v 11). But the end of Revelation warns us what will happen to faithless cowards, who would rather deny Christ than face suffering: "Their portion will be in the lake that burns with fire and sulfur, which is the second death" (21 v 8).

Someone who held on to this promise of the crown of life was Polycarp, Bishop of Smyrna. Around the year 155, some 60 years after this letter was written, Polycarp was told by the governing authorities to bow down to Caesar and to renounce Christ. Polycarp responded, "For 86 years I have been his servant, and he has done me no wrong. How can I blaspheme my King, who saved me?" The proconsul then threatened Polycarp with wild beasts and fire. Again, Polycarp responded, "You threaten with a fire that burns only briefly and after just a little while is extinguished, for you are ignorant of the fire of the coming judgment and eternal punishment, which is reserved for the ungodly." Then he added, "But why do you delay? Come, do what you wish."

Polycarp, an 86-year-old Christian, essentially says… *Bring it on!* Can you imagine that? Oh, how I long for that kind of faith in all my moments of cowardice! But Jesus says that we can have it. It requires that we see him in all his glory—the risen Christ who, as the first and the last, rules over every moment. He's the One who died and rose again to die no more. When we look to this risen Christ, and believe what he has promised us, then we will not be afraid. That is the faith of Polycarp, and that is the faith I want. That is the faith we should all want. That is the faith we should pray for.

So, in the (almost) words of Polycarp... bring it on!

DANGER THREE

COMPROMISE

12 And to the angel of the church in Pergamum write: "The words of him who has the sharp two-edged sword.

13 "I know where you dwell, where Satan's throne is. Yet you hold fast my name, and you did not deny my faith even in the days of Antipas my faithful witness, who was killed among you, where Satan dwells. 14 But I have a few things against you: you have some there who hold the teaching of Balaam, who taught Balak to put a stumbling block before the sons of Israel, so that they might eat food sacrificed to idols and practice sexual immorality. 15 So also you have some who hold the teaching of the Nicolaitans. 16 Therefore repent. If not, I will come to you soon and war against them with the sword of my mouth. 17 He who has an ear, let him hear what the Spirit says to the churches. To the one who conquers I will give some of the hidden manna, and I will give him a white stone, with a new name written on the stone that no one knows except the one who receives it."

Revelation 2 v 12-17

W e're living in a brave new world of changing cultural values—and if you do not conform, you will be punished.

In this brave new world, it is a hate crime to affirm publicly that God ordained marriage as a covenant relationship between one man and one woman for life. In this brave new world, it is anti-woman to believe the baby inside a mother's womb is a person. In this brave new world, it is intolerant to hold that gender identity is defined by the God who created us male and female. In this brave new world, it is anti-science to acknowledge our universe as an orderly creation by an omnipotent God.

And to protect our brave new world from all who continue to worship an antiquated deity—such as the God of the Bible—Western governments enact laws that ensure we all bow down before the culture's postmodern idols in their newfound temples. There is no room for postmodern "atheists"—*not* believing in our culture's newly emerging values is simply not an option. So all who fail to hold fast to the new cultural commandments will be punished:

- On June 15, 2017, Tim Farron, a professing evangelical Christian, resigned as leader of Britain's Liberal Democrats amid pressure from his political party because his Christian convictions made him the subject of suspicion. When he stepped down he explained that, "To be a political leader—especially of a progressive, liberal party in 2017—and to live as a committed Christian, to hold faithfully to the Bible's teaching, has felt impossible for me."

- In July of 2012, Jack Phillips, a professing evangelical Christian and owner of Masterpiece Cakeshop in Lakewood, Colorado, U.S.A., refused to provide a wedding cake for a gay couple, arguing that to do so would be the same as taking part in the celebration and affirming gay marriage. From 2013 to 2016, Mr. Phillips has argued his religious rights before Colorado courts and the Colorado Civil Rights Commission, but they have argued that the gay couple's civil rights trump his religious rights.

- In February 2017, Robert Hudson, a teacher and coach who led the Fellowship of Christian Athletes at a California High School, was told that he would be dismissed at the end of the school year, shortly before receiving tenure. "The only thing I can think of is that I am being harassed about my faith in Jesus Christ." Hudson says his only conflict with the school was when he was formally reprimanded for questioning the principal when asked to remove various Christian-inspired quotes from his classroom.

Christian, this is the world we live in, and it looks as though these cultural pressures are only going to increase. And this presents us, our churches, and our pastors with a very real danger—that we compromise our beliefs just to fit in and avoid harassment.

In many ways this danger bears some similarities to what we saw in the previous chapter. And perhaps as you're reading, it's all starting to sound a bit alarmist. *I would never deny Christ or abandon the faith*, you think to yourself. While Christians suffer in faraway places like Somalia, Iran, or China, you're in small-town Nebraska, or tolerant London, or progressive Paris. Yet while we may not deny Christ altogether, there's a creeping temptation for us to adapt his claims to suit our culture and, if we're in a position of influence, to lead our churches to do so as well.

Church history has shown us that if we don't keep our guard up, we will fall prey to compromising what we believe in any number of little ways that snowball out of control. One example is the Fundamentalist-Modernist Controversy of the early 20th century, when, among other things, leaders of mainline denominations led their churches to adapt the Bible to the theory of evolution in order to be in line with the scientific thought of their day. Consequently, over time these "modernist" leaders convinced their churches to question the inspiration and authority of the Bible, leading to a denial of the virgin birth, the deity of Christ, and the resurrection.

"Ah, but that's *them*!" we may think, "There's no way *I* would ever compromise on what I believe!" But to think that we're immune from compromise is both proud and foolish. For one thing, the secular thought-police are ever so aggressive in making sure our views align with contemporary culture. But the danger is more subtle than that too. Secular culture is the air that we breathe—as we read books and watch films and scroll Twitter, we're inhaling a particular worldview, and it's changing us in ways that we're often blind to. Today we are being challenged on the place of faith in the public sphere and whether there is any such thing as objective truth at all, and no longer just on the existence of God and the exclusivity of salvation through Christ alone (although these objections remain too).

And these doctrinal clashes—what we believe versus what our secular culture believes—will only continue to challenge the church. After all, this danger has been around since the church's birth—it's what Jesus warned his church in Pergamum against two millennia ago. Several times in Revelation 2 v 12-17 Jesus uses the language of "hold fast to" and "faith" or "teaching." The emphasis of this third message is the danger of not "holding fast" to Jesus and his teaching ("my faith," v 13).

Jesus could not be clearer: the road to judgment is paved with hundreds of little daily doctrinal compromises.

Seeing the Sword-Wielder

Once again, Jesus begins his message by identifying himself with a description from chapter one that is specific to the needs of that local church. In 1 v 16 John saw Jesus with "a sharp two-edged sword" coming from his mouth. We're reminded that the words the church in Pergamum are about to receive are not just any words; they are "the words of him who has the sharp two-edged sword" (2 v 12). Now, Jesus doesn't literally have a sword coming out of his mouth. This image indicates that Jesus is the ruler, the just judge, and—crucially—that he judges by his word. When Jesus returns and the day of judgment finally arrives, he will judge by the very standard he has already spoken in his word, our Bible. There will be no surprises; no one will have a legitimate excuse. Jesus, the living Word, by which the Father created all things, is also the Word of God, by which all things will be judged (19 v 11-16). Here's the point: Jesus, who has the sword, has the ultimate authority to judge and to rule.

Why does Jesus emphasize this? Well, elsewhere in the New Testament we learn that God has given human rulers and governments "the sword" of justice "to punish those who do evil and praise those who do good" (Romans 13 v 1-7; 1 Peter 2 v 14). God ordained that human governments reflect his authority on earth. Earthly authority can certainly be abused—and it was for the Pergamum Christians—but that doesn't undo the fact that God has ordered his world in relationships of authority and submission. Yet while human rulers wield the sword of earthly justice, the ultimate sword-wielder is Jesus—and where the two are in conflict, we owe our obedience to Jesus.

So Jesus identifies himself in contrast to earthly Caesars, rulers, kings, queens, presidents, and governors. While the earthly government wields the sword of earthly justice, Jesus is the risen Christ, who wields the sword of true, righteous, divine justice, and he will come again to judge the living and the dead by the word that comes from his mouth.

Two swords. Two types of justice. But the questions is: which sword will we fear?

You see, that's the choice we will face when the cold steel of the government's sword is laid to our necks. Which sword do you fear?

Of course, the official sword of government is often supported by the unofficial court of public opinion. In fact, in the West at least, it's often public opinion that drives the government's agenda. This is what's happening in the religious liberty battles in the United States right now. Whether it's the news media, Hollywood movies, or just our friends on Facebook, the unofficial court of public opinion is always in session—and we will face its "sword" too. In those moments, when the court of public opinion decrees that our beliefs are bigoted, intolerant, and "on the wrong side of history," which sword will we fear? Will you give in to appease the judges before you, or will you stand fast?

With pressures like these, it's no wonder that our churches face the danger that, to save our own lives, or even just to fit in, we might fail to hold firmly to Jesus and his teaching. This is the danger of doctrinal compromise.

I Know Where You Live

The Christians in Pergamum lived in a world where the sword that God gave to Caesar had been corrupted by Satanic influence. "I know where you dwell," says Jesus, "where Satan's throne is" (2 v 13a). Later in Revelation, we're told that Satan shares his throne with the beast (13 v 2; 16 v 10), which represents tyrannical government (13 v 1-4; see also Daniel 7 v 1-8). Pergamum was the capital city for the Roman province of Asia. As this city was the seat of government, Satan used it as his instrument in his to attempt to destroy the church (Revelation 12 v 17).

Pergamum also served as a center for emperor worship, while also housing various other temples to important Greco-Roman deities. These gods demanded worship in exchange for a productive and peaceful social order. Asclepius, the god of healing (represented by the serpent even to this day in medical insignia), promised health and healing. Athena, the goddess of war, promised victory. Demeter, the goddess of the harvest, promised a fertile earth. And Dionysus, the god of wine and patron of the arts, promised joy, ecstasy, and debauchery. But above all these deities stood Zeus, the god of all gods. Pergamum was home to the great altar of Zeus, the savior.

In addition, each god or goddess was related to a specific vocation or guild. To gain acceptance in these local guilds and to be able to trade, you had to participate in the worship of "your" deity. Imagine the social pressure Christians were under to practice idolatry, just to be able to work, to support their family, to simply survive. Throughout Revelation, Jesus shows how these pagan religions, represented by the imagery of the false prophet, work in tandem with the corrupt government (the beast) to attempt to destroy the people of God (for example, 16 v 13).

As it turns out, our world is neither brave nor new. Today, Satan continues to corrupt human governments. As instruments of Satan, instead of using the sword to punish evil and promote good, these governments punish good and promote evil—in some regards at least. Consider how a government might turn the sword of earthly justice against the people of God. Think about how some governments pressure us to accept their definitions of marriage, sexuality, and gender. And mere acceptance is barely enough—they expect us to celebrate their commandments and bow down in worship to the beast. And if we refuse, we are labeled cultural "atheists" and punished. If social ostracism isn't enough to bring us to our knees in adoration, then legal action must be taken. Again, the question is: which sword will we fear?

Many of the Christians in Pergamum feared the sword of Jesus, and Jesus commends them for that. His words in 2 v 13 are wonderfully reassuring: he knows their situation, and he understands the social and cultural pressures related to living "where Satan's throne is," and he commends them for staying faithful. Despite the fact that they live in the satanic capital, Jesus says they "hold fast [to] my name, and you did not deny my faith even in the days of Antipas my faithful witness, who was killed among you, where Satan dwells." Whoever Antipas was, he lived in Pergamum and was a faithful witness—in other words, a martyr. He held fast to Jesus and his teaching, but it cost him his life. Clearly, if Antipas could be killed for his faith, so could the other Christians in Pergamum. And yet, knowing of Antipas' fate, these believers in Pergamum remained steadfast in their faith.

Pressured or Persuaded?

"But," Jesus continues, "I have a few things against you: you have some there who hold the teaching of Balaam" (2 v 14). Jesus is alluding to the time in Israel's history when Balak, king of Moab—an enemy nation—hired the prophet Balaam to curse Israel (Numbers 22 – 24). Much to King Balak's frustration, God intervened so that Balaam was only able to pronounce blessings, not curses, on Israel. But Balak and the Moabites found another way to cause Israel's undoing. While the Israelites were camped on the plains of Moab, they "began to whore with the daughters of Moab." Then, on Balaam's advice, the women of Moab invited the Israelites "to the sacrifices of their gods, and the people ate and bowed down to their gods" (Numbers 25 v 1-2; 31 v 16). As a result, God sent a plague that killed 24,000 Israelites. This is the incident Jesus is referring to when he says that the prophet Balaam "taught Balak to put a stumbling block before the sons of Israel, so that they might eat food sacrificed to idols and practice sexual immorality" (Revelation 2 v 14).

And now Jesus says that there are some Christians in Pergamum who "hold" to Balaam's teaching. Clearly, some Christians in Pergamum were participating in pagan festivals where they too ate food sacrificed to idols and engaged in sexual immorality. And perhaps we can sympathize. Keep in mind that to fit into the social fabric and earn a living, the citizens of Pergamum had to pay homage to the deities related to their guilds. And in relation to the Roman gods, the ultimate test of allegiance was to bow down and acknowledge Caesar as Lord. Those who refused were punished, tortured, and perhaps, like Antipas, even killed. No wonder it seemed easier to go along to get along.

In the West today, we likely won't be killed for our faith, but the temptation to compromise is still very real. In science class, you may be tempted to compromise on the doctrine of creation and embrace Darwinian evolutionary biology if you want an A grade. In academia, you may be tempted to compromise on the doctrine of Scripture if you're to have any hope of receiving tenure. In counseling, you may be tempted to compromise on the doctrine of sin if you expect to receive certification from a governing agency. In the workplace, you may be tempted to compromise on the doctrine of marriage and celebrate same-sex relationships if you want to keep your job or the boss's friendship. I could go on and on and on. The point is that every day we are tempted in a thousand little ways to cave in and just go along to get along. Whether you're a pastor or a professor, a public school teacher or a politician, a supervisor or a subordinate, a public figure or a private citizen, the pressure is increasing, both from our culture and our government, to compromise. Pause to reflect long enough and honestly enough, and you'll know where the pressure comes for you.

But doctrinal compromise isn't always the result of cultural pressure—sometimes it comes from cultural persuasion. Jesus goes on: "So also you have some who hold the teaching of the Nicolaitans" (v 15). Here he connects the teaching of Balaam with the teaching of the Nicolaitans; it appears that the Nicolaitans within the church legitimized Christian participation in pagan practices. It seems that not all Christians in Pergamum practiced idolatry against their conscience; some may have done so willingly, having been convinced by the teaching of the Nicolaitans.

Such doctrinal compromises result from little bits of our faith being chipped away by the "false prophets" of our age. Think of the Christian university student who arrives at school committed to sexual purity, only to be convinced by her "Christian" boyfriend that it is completely acceptable to express their love for one another through sexual intimacy. It's easy for such compromises to take hold of whole churches too. Consider the church that receives a new pastor trained at a prestigious seminary, who begins to teach that the "traditional" view of hell is nothing but a medieval fantasy. This pastor uses the Bible to make his case, and his arguments seem reasonable. After all, how can a God of love send so many people to an eternity of torment?

Sometimes the change in our doctrinal convictions emerges out of our personal experiences. A family in the church raises their children in the discipline and instruction of the Lord, but at 22 years of age, their oldest son declares that he is homosexual and wants them to come to his "wedding" and bless his union with his long-time partner. His parents can see that they make each other happy—in so many ways they seem good together. Or maybe it's the family whose 16-year-old daughter reveals—with obvious emotional distress—that deep down she feels male, not female. She tearfully asks her parents to recognize who she really is. Rather than calling her Christina, she now wants them to call her Christopher.

There is no question or doubt over the love these families have for their children, and the pull of emotions is compelling. So if they are not clear about what the Bible teaches concerning God's creation of humanity as male and female, they will be susceptible to the teachings of the "Nicolaitans" of our day who urge them to "get with the times," lest they be "on the wrong side of history." As hard as it is to remain faithful in these situations, we have no options but to hold fast, with grace and compassion, to the teaching of Jesus.

So then, by holding to the teaching of the Nicolaitans, whether by pressure or persuasion, some believers in Pergamum had compromised their faith. And we face this pressure too—that we would compromise the faith either because we fear the sword of the government and the court of public opinion, or because we've become convinced by the false prophets of our age, or our own experience. When our faith is challenged, will we continue to believe that Jesus' words are true and good, or will we turn to the words of someone else?

New Mind, Fresh Start

Admit it; you've caved in. I'll admit it; I've caved in. If we find ourselves in the place of doctrinal compromise, Jesus has two words for us: "Therefore repent" (v 16).

This call is one of patience and kindness—throughout the Old and New Testaments, "repent" is a word of hope, telling us that no matter how far off course we've gone, there is still opportunity to return to God. Some people have explained repentance as an about-face: when going in one direction, away from God, to turn around and begin going in the opposite direction, toward God. But before we can change direction, we must become convinced that we're going in the wrong direction. The word Jesus uses for "repent" literally means to change your mind. Repentance means changing your thinking, or renewing your mind. This is what Jesus calls us to do. If you fear the sword of the government, change your way of thinking. If you're being persuaded away from the faith, renew your mind.

How? With the very word that Jesus has revealed: his teaching, the word of the gospel, what we call "the faith." Your mind is not a vacuum. The only way to change your mind is to replace wrong ways of thinking with the true ways of thinking: about Christ, about the gospel, about the faith, and about both the pressures and persuasions threatening your faith. And if we are church leaders, it is crucial to equip our church members to change their minds too. We must not preach from the lofty heights of an ivory tower. It's vital that we understand—*really* understand—the pulls and pressures affecting our flock; and then call people to repent where they've got it wrong.

Ultimately, what all of us need is a bigger view of Jesus: the all-glorious, risen Christ. He has a double-edged sword coming from his mouth. You may fear the sword of the beastly government now, but Jesus "will come to you soon and war against [the "Nicolaitans" and all idolatrous doctrinal compromisers] with the sword of [his] mouth" (v 16).

When Jesus says this, the background of the Old Testament incident of Baal worship is likely still in view. In Numbers 31 v 3, Moses declared, "Arm men from among you for the war, that they may go against Midian to execute the Lord's vengeance on Midian." Midian experienced God's sword at the hands of the Israelites because they, in partnership with Moab, were also responsible for putting a stumbling block before the people of Israel that led them to idolatry (Numbers 22 v 4, 7). Likewise, the Nicolaitans put a stumbling block before the church in Pergamum that led them to idolatry. So it is Jesus himself who will come with his sword and make war against the Nicolaitans and all who fail to hold fast to him and his teaching. We are meant to fear Jesus' sword, not that of earthly governments. By leaving us with the imagery of this final battle against all idolaters, Jesus means to impress upon us the dread of the day when he comes wielding his sword.

But Jesus doesn't seek to change our minds only with an image of judgment that will keep us up at night. He also leaves us with two images that will make us long for heaven in order to encourage faithfulness now.

A Better Invitation

The promise of the risen Christ in each message is just what each church needs to remember, cling to, and hope in, as they face their danger. To the Christians in Pergamum who are tempted to participate in the pagan banquets, Jesus first promises that "to the one who conquers I will give some of the hidden manna" (Revelation 2 v 17). In Jewish tradition, it is said that Jeremiah gathered the tent, the altar of incense, and the ark containing a jar of manna, and hid them on Mount Sinai to keep them safe from the invading Babylonians. These would be revealed and given to the people when the Messiah returned. Hidden manna, then, points the church in Pergamum to the messianic banquet, the marriage supper of the Lamb. If we hold fast to the faith, we will often be left out of the world's celebrations. Rather than feel excluded, long for the marriage supper of the Lamb, the feast where we will dine at the King's table.

Second, the risen Christ also promises "a white stone" (v 17). The word for stone indicates that Jesus is speaking of a small pebble. Victors in athletic games received white pebbles in order to gain entrance into celebratory banquets. If that's what Jesus means, then it is possible, and perhaps even likely, that the white stone serves as an official invitation permitting entrance into this messianic banquet. Currently, Christians are made to feel that we're on the losing side of history, but Jesus reminds us that all who endure are victors! And all victors will gain entrance into the celebration at the King's table when history comes to its conclusion in Christ.

Finally, all who hold fast to Jesus and his teaching will receive "a new name" written on the white pebble—this likely indicates the new identity we have in Christ. Because we are now called by a new name—Jesus' name—we are the people of God. And because we bear Jesus' name, we will be allowed entrance into the messianic banquet. As we hold fast to Jesus and his gospel, our name in this world will be dragged through the mud. But have no fear, Christian—you hold a white stone in your hand.

So look forward, and stand firm.

¹⁸ And to the angel of the church in Thyatira write: "The words of the Son of God, who has eyes like a flame of fire, and whose feet are like burnished bronze.

¹⁹ "I know your works, your love and faith and service and patient endurance, and that your latter works exceed the first. ²⁰ But I have this against you, that you tolerate that woman Jezebel, who calls herself a prophetess and is teaching and seducing my servants to practice sexual immorality and to eat food sacrificed to idols. ²¹ I gave her time to repent, but she refuses to repent of her sexual immorality. ²² Behold, I will throw her onto a sickbed, and those who commit adultery with her I will throw into great tribulation, unless they repent of her works, ²³ and I will strike her children dead. And all the churches will know that I am he who searches mind and heart, and I will give to each of you according to your works. ²⁴ But to the rest of you in Thyatira, who do not hold this teaching, who have not learned what some call the deep things of Satan, to you I say, I do not lay on you any other burden. ²⁵ Only hold fast what you have until I come. ²⁶ The one who conquers and who keeps my works until the end, to him I will give authority over the nations, ²⁷ and he will rule them with a rod of iron, as when earthen pots are broken in pieces, even as I myself have received authority from my Father. ²⁸ And I will give him the morning star. ²⁹ He who has an ear, let him hear what the Spirit says to the churches."

Revelation 2 v 18-29

Tensions ran high. Several members made assumptions; some spread gossip; most took sides. As a result, church conflict erupted.

To address the increasing fracture, I addressed the congregation on a Sunday evening to explain the biblical process for resolving personal conflict over sins committed by a brother or sister. Because the church had never practiced church discipline, I walked them through Matthew 18 v 15-20, point by point, appealing for the necessity for godly and gracious confrontation for the sake of the gospel, the soul of the sinner, the unity of the church, our witness in the community, and the glory of Christ.

That's when he stood up. He was a deacon and long-time member of the church. We had all just met beforehand, myself and the deacons, to make sure we were on the same page. Yet, when I finished my comments, he stood up to speak. "I don't know about what you just said," he boldly declared, "but here's how I feel..." He intimated that I was making a fuss over nothing, and that the real problem was me. He allowed his personal feelings for the person in unrepentant sin to rule over Scripture. I was dumbfounded. I didn't know how to respond. While believing the Bible and having previously agreed on its application, this deacon chose tolerance over church discipline, solely based on his "feelings."

As a young pastor, I learned a valuable lesson about church members that night. Generally, churches strive to love Christ, love one another, and honor their pastor. Largely, we believe the Bible, seek to obey its commands, and follow its guidance. Regularly, we speak out against cultural degradation, stand up against secular sins, and pass judgment on worldly morality. But when it comes to speaking the hard truths of the Bible to those we love—namely, ourselves, our family, or our friends—we are far too often willing to tolerate sin. For whatever reason—whether it's loyalty, deception, or fear of man—we are reluctant to confront the people we love and expose their error. You know, "judge not, lest ye be judged," and all that. But the danger is that to avoid conflict or to maintain a relationship, we tolerate unrepentant sin in the church.

Admittedly, in our wider culture "tolerance" is heralded as a virtue. The mark of a modern society is to live and let live—to accept and affirm everyone's beliefs and behaviors. For Christians, the word often has more negative connotations. It feels as if "tolerance" is used as a trump card against those who don't embrace the progressive ideas and morals of secular culture. Today, you're "intolerant" if you suggest sex should be reserved for marriage, if you refuse to acknowledge the man who now identifies as a woman, or if you believe that Jesus is the only way to God.

But the focus of this next message in Revelation, and of this chapter, is not on tolerating people who are "out there," but people who are "in here"—people who claim to belong to the body of Christ, but who act otherwise. Within the church, we're not to tolerate sin. Jesus wants us to take sin seriously. He speaks about "cutting off" our hands and feet and "tearing out" our eyes if they cause us to sin (Matthew 18 v 7-9). Jesus is purposely using shocking language, but he makes his point. Do not tolerate sin: in ourselves, in our brothers and sisters, in the church. Instead, we must speak the truth in love to our unrepentant brothers and sisters. We must not leave them in their sin or expect others to leave us in ours.

Why? Because one day they and we will meet Jesus. And not the kind of Jesus you meet in picture books...

No Sunday School Jesus

As with the messages to the other churches, the Thyatirans can only begin to overcome the danger of tolerance by looking at the risen Christ. Jesus identifies himself in Revelation 2 v 18 as "the Son of God." This title is a reference to Psalm 2, which reminds us that Jesus is the royal Son whom God has placed on David's throne as ruler and judge over all the world.

Additionally, Jesus says he "has eyes like a flame of fire," and his "feet are like burnished bronze" (Revelation 2 v 18, just as in 1 v 14-15). This imagery echoes Daniel 10, where God's messenger, who makes war against the rebellious nations, is similarly described (Daniel 10 v 6, 13, 20-21). So overall, this description points toward judgment. Jesus is the Son to whom God the Father has given authority to judge. Nothing escapes his fiery gaze (Revelation 2 v 18)—he is able to search "mind and heart" and "will give to each of you according to your works" (v 23). As for those who rebel against him, he will crush them under his hard, metallic feet.

This is not your Sunday-school Jesus! This Jesus is frightening; he's meant to be. He wants us to realize that it is better for unrepentant sinners to fall under the discipline of brothers and sisters now, than to fall under the just judgment of the returning Christ. This vision of Jesus is also meant to keep us from sin. We may think that no one will ever know when we click on that pornographic website or lust after our workmate or think envious thoughts about our neighbor. But Jesus knows; he sees everything.

If we're to overcome the danger of tolerance, we must see Jesus for who he is: the all-glorious King and Judge of all the earth. A day is coming when every knee will bow and every tongue will confess that Jesus Christ is Lord. So the message is: be wise and bow down to King Jesus now; serve him with fear; and kiss the Son (Psalm 2 v 10-12).

The Trouble with Love over Truth

The church in Thyatira was full of love. In fact, Jesus highlights their love by listing it as the first of their works, even before faith, service, and patient endurance (Revelation 2 v 19). Who wouldn't want to belong to a church like this—a church of whom Jesus says, *You're growing in love, faith, service, and patient endurance*? I wish that all our churches could be described like that! But no church is perfect. And neither was the one in Thyatira.

The problem was that the church emphasized love to the neglect of doctrinal purity. This is the opposite problem to that of the church in Ephesus. The church in Ephesus emphasized truth over love, but the church in Thyatira emphasized love over truth. And once again, we see the danger of separating the two. This skewed emphasis led the Thyatiran Christians to tolerate a false prophetess who was encouraging idolatry (v 20).

Thyatira was not a particularly important city like Ephesus or Pergamum, but like them, it was still marked by idolatry. The prominent deity in Thyatira was Apollo, son of Zeus, which may be one reason why Jesus identifies himself as the "Son of God" in verse 18. Apollo was known as a god of healing, whether by his own hand or that of his son Asclepius, but he was also known to bring sickness and plague on those who angered him.

Like Pergamum, Thyatira also had trade guilds connected with the Greco-Roman deities. But because of the prominence of such guilds in Thyatira, they would have posed a great threat to the church's faithfulness. The commentator Barry Beitzel observes that "the trade guilds held periodic festivals in which food offered to idols was consumed. This was sometimes accompanied by licentious rites in which religion and sex were mingled." (*Baker Encyclopedia of the Bible*, Vol 2, p 2059)

Though we may not go to pagan temples today, many Christians face similar pressures. Imagine a Christian university student who is a member of a fraternity or sorority. They might attend a party that begins in celebratory fashion, but, as the bottles get emptier and the night gets longer, it turns into debauchery and sexual immorality. *Come on, don't be such a prude...* Or think of a Christian business-person whose company rewards their team with a trip, but, over the weekend getaway, their peers pressure them into experimenting with marijuana or cocaine. *Come on, no one's going to get hurt...* Or perhaps a believer wants to be inducted into a social society or club, but they quickly learn that the initiation rites involve actual pagan rituals. *Come on, it doesn't really mean anything...* In such cases, the pressure to obtain or retain a status within your "guild" is a very real danger.

Yet the bigger problem for the church in Thyatira was a woman who, claiming to be a prophetess, legitimized such behavior. And in fact, the still-bigger problem was that the church tolerated her (v 20). Like Jezebel in 1 Kings 16 v 31-32, who led Israel's King Ahab to serve and worship Baal, this woman led some in the church to idolatry through her teaching. We don't know the exact content of her teaching, but judging from the ironic statement in Revelation 2 v 24 in which Jesus calls her teaching "the deep things of Satan," it's likely she offered some type of "deeper knowledge" that "freed" Christians to participate in pagan feasts. This Thyatiran "Jezebel" likely taught a perverted version of Christian freedom.

Jesus' description is both subtle and clear. She is like Jezebel, but, by "[calling] herself a prophetess," she claimed to be speaking with authority from God. How often do we hear such claims today: men and women, on television and radio, through books and conferences, who claim direct revelation from God? They claim a "deeper knowledge of God," and they're willing to share it with you... for a price. But these modern-day "prophets" don't all look like religious whackos who claim to have been to heaven and come back again. Some appear credible: a flurry of experts with Ph.D.s and pastors with huge churches, who claim to have understood the Bible in a way previously unknown through most of church history—and they want to teach you so you too may become liberated. Some want to liberate you from antiquated views of marriage, gender, and sexuality. Some want to liberate you from a restrictive view of God's salvation in Christ alone. Some want to liberate you from an abusive understanding of the atonement. Some want to liberate you from a "legalistic" view of holiness. Modern-day Jezebels are gifted in making the beautiful doctrines revealed by God in Scripture appear stifling, restrictive, and limiting.

I sometimes wonder whether we Christians are some of the most gullible people on the face of the earth. I remember talking to a professing Christian who claimed he no longer needed to ask for forgiveness. "Jesus' sacrifice is so great," he told me, "that when you repent of your sins and trust Christ for the first time, that's all the repentance that is necessary." So I asked him, "Are you telling me that if you commit adultery against your wife, you don't need to repent and ask her forgiveness?" He said, "Nope! Jesus has already forgiven me." Later, I learned he was reading a book by a radio personality whose teaching "liberated" him from a life of ongoing repentance.

If we're not satisfied with the normal Christian life—a life that's about the thousand daily steps of faithfulness—we look for a "Christianity" that's more radical, more mysterious, more exciting, and more liberating. And for as long as we crave "deeper knowledge," there will be plenty of "Jezebels" out there, both male and female, to provide it. And if we're not careful, in our quest for "deeper knowledge," we ourselves may become that Jezebel: "having the appearance of godliness, but denying its power … always learning and never able to arrive at a knowledge of the truth" (2 Timothy 3 v 5, 7).

Or maybe you *are* satisfied with the simple, authentic gospel, and you're pretty good at sniffing out the Jezebels from the genuine. Great! But do you love your weaker brothers and sisters enough to protect *them* from today's Jezebels too? Are you prepared to address and, when required, confront "Jezebels" in your church who are leading others into sin? After all, it's the Christians who tolerate the Jezebels whom Jesus calls out first (Revelation 2 v 20). We must overcome a fear of hurt feelings or lost relationships. We must overcome a fear of rejection or public ridicule. And pastors, we must overcome a fear of losing members and contributions.

How do we overcome such fears? By believing—*really* believing—that it is better for our unrepentant brothers and sisters to fall under our rebuke and discipline than to fall under the judgment of the risen King. And so it's to that theme that Jesus returns next.

Four Truths about Judgment

Often, when we think of rebuke or church discipline, we wrongly think of unreasonable harshness, unfair decisions, and overbearing—or even hateful—leaders. That might be because we've been in churches where this has indeed been the case. But that's not how God does discipline, and it shouldn't be how we do discipline either.

Notice the kindness of the Lord in verse 21: "I gave her time to repent." In "Jezebel's" case, it appears that she had been sufficiently warned. Perhaps some in the church had confronted her at one point, but when she didn't listen, they allowed her to continue leading other members into idolatry. Sadly, in verse 21 we also see the hardness of an unrepentant heart, for "she refuses to repent of her sexual immorality." We tend to forget that God's judgment always comes after his grace and mercy have been spurned. And now Jesus' patience has come to an end. Since the church has refused to discipline Jezebel, Jesus will now take matters into his own hands. In the verses that follow, Jesus reveals four truths about his judgment.

First, Jesus' judgment will be severe (v 22a). He "will throw her onto a sickbed." The imagery Jesus uses here is one of spiritual unfaithfulness. The real prophets spoke of God's relationship to his people as a marital covenant, and their unfaithfulness to God as prostitution and adultery (Ezekiel 16; Hosea 1 – 3). So too here. Because Jezebel encouraged the people of God to "commit adultery" with pagan deities, Jesus will throw her onto a "bed" or "stretcher." To clarify the image, the English Standard Version calls it a "sickbed." We don't normally associate God's judgment with physical sickness and suffering, but the idea is not foreign to the Bible. In 1 Corinthians 11 v 30, the apostle Paul reminds the Corinthians that some of them are "weak and ill, and some have died," because of God's judgment due to their abuse of the Lord's Supper. Ultimately, all sin leads to death—but God does not judge all sin with immediate death. Still, for Jezebel, this seems to be what is coming. And these earthly judgments are little foretastes of what will one day come in full.

Second, Jesus' judgment will be thorough (Revelation 2 v 22b-23a). Jezebel will not face judgment alone. All "those who commit adultery with her," declares Jesus, "I will throw into great tribulation," and "I will strike her children [that is, her followers] dead." Gullibility does not excuse us from judgment. Each of us is responsible for our own actions: "Everyone shall die for his own iniquity" (Jeremiah 31 v 30).

And yet, so long as we have breath and the King has not returned, Jesus gives opportunity to repent. All that Jezebel's "children" need to do to escape the coming King's judgment is to "repent of her works" (Revelation 2 v 22)—that is, change their minds about Jezebel's teaching, and embrace Jesus' teaching instead. But if they do not repent, judgment is inevitable, and it will be thorough.

Third, Jesus' judgment will be just (v 23). He "will give to each of you according to your works." Because Jesus has "eyes like a flame of fire" (v 18), he "searches mind and heart" (v 23). He sees all and knows all. In Revelation 20 v 12, we see an image of final judgment where books, apparently containing a record of all human deeds, are opened: "And the dead were judged by what was written in the books, according to what they had done." Nothing gets past Jesus' gaze, so he will judge according to all he has seen of our lives: our thoughts, attitudes, and actions. He is in possession of all the facts, so it will be perfectly fair.

Fourth, Jesus' judgment will display his power, authority, and glory (2 v 23). The consequence of Jezebel's judgment is that "all the churches will know that [Jesus] is he who searches mind and heart, and [who] will give to each of you according to your works." In other words, Jesus' judgment will show that, as God's Son, he has been given authority to judge in a way that is severe, thorough, and just.

This is a warning to all who do not hold fast to Jesus and his teaching. With this simple but terrifying knowledge of God and his Son, why would you not bow down and kiss the Son?

The One Things Jesus Wants

So, reject modern-day "Jezebels" and their idolatries. "I do not lay on you any other burden," says Jesus, than to throw off idols and hold fast to him (v 24-25). Our idols today may not be made of wood, stone, or metal, but they are no less real. They may be more subtle, but they are no less dangerous. All idolatry begins in the heart and only later does it manifest itself outwardly, whether in statues or desires and behaviors. In essence, idols offer competing promises of joy and satisfaction—will we find joy and satisfaction in God or sex, God or money, God or power, God or food?

Behind all our unrepentant sin is a turning away from God as our sole source of joy and satisfaction, and a turning to find satisfaction in our preferred idols. Both the wife manipulating her husband and the husband who abuses his wife are bowing down to the idol of control. The workaholic who craves money and possessions will sacrifice his family at the altar of wealth. The family who prioritizes sports on a Sunday at the expense of church commitment is worshiping at the shrine of freedom. And the single Christian who starts dating a non-Christian is fulfilling their desire to feel loved and wanted as the ultimate source of their joy and satisfaction. Sadly, many modern-day Jezebels encourage and legitimize Christians and churches to find their joy and satisfaction in these false gods.

But again, we don't just need to watch out for ourselves. Remember, the danger in Thyatira was that *the church tolerated* a false teacher and her idolatry. As a result, those who stayed faithful were allowing some of their brothers and sisters to reject Jesus and wander into his judgment. Jesus' warnings help us to see the corporate nature of the church. It is not loving to watch our brothers and sisters wander into Jesus' judgment without warning them. We bear responsibility for one another.

One side of the coin is to "consider how to stir up one another to love and good works, not neglecting to meet together, as is the habit of some, but encouraging one another, and all the more as you see the Day drawing near" (Hebrews 10 v 24-25).

But there's another side of the coin too. Jesus' concern is that the church would "hold fast what you have until I come" (Revelation 2 v 25). And all who do will share in his rule: "The one who conquers and who keeps my works until the end, to him I will give authority over the nations, and he will rule them with a rod of iron, as when earthen pots are broken in pieces, even as I myself have received authority from my Father" (v 26-27). Through our union with Christ, we are royal sons and daughters (1 v 6; 5 v 10; 20 v 6). And as part of that, one of our roles is judgment. The church has received authority to judge alongside Jesus. Paul argues that because Christians will one day "judge the world," we should be able to judge "matters pertaining to this life" between brothers and sisters in Christ (1 Corinthians 6 v 2-3). As a church, then, we share in Christ's rule by exercising the authority he's given us in the practice of church discipline.

But we're to do this in a way that reflects Christ's patience and fairness. Remember, we are to "speak the truth *in love*" (Ephesians 4 v 15). For church members, this means maintaining the dignity of the person who's sinned against you or gone astray. You don't gossip to others about them; you go to the person—one to one (Matthew 18 v 15). Don't make blunt accusations. Instead, approach the person in love and humility. Remember, the goal is to win your brother or sister, not the argument. Whenever I've had to confront a church member, I've found it's helpful to begin by asking questions. I'll never possess Christ's perfect knowledge, but asking open questions instead of jumping to conclusions goes a long way. "Are you OK? I've noticed awkwardness between us. Have I done something to offend you?" If the confrontation is more doctrinally related, I might say, "I've noticed you're posting videos on Facebook from John Doe's ministry regarding a proposed date for the return of Christ. How did you become interested in his stuff? Are you familiar with what Jesus says about us not knowing the day or hour of his return? Would you be willing to sit down with me and talk about this?"

When confronting a Christian brother or sister, we hope they will repent and can be reconciled to us. When they do repent, we must freely forgive them—we must not hold long-past sins over their heads like a dagger. We must show grace. But sometimes they continue in their sin or error without repenting. It is only then that we include other brothers and sisters in the rescue operation (Matthew 18 v 16). Ultimately, if they still refuse to listen and repent, we must ultimately make the entire church aware, hoping that by engaging the entire church, one of us will be able to get through to them (v 17). Sadly, there will be occasions where they will even refuse to listen to the church. In such cases—where it concerns indisputable matters and not secondary issues of doctrine (see Romans 14)—we remove them from membership because they are not living according to their profession of faith in Christ (Matthew 18 v 18).

Because the loving process of church discipline is rarely practiced today, leaders must teach and equip the church to enact it. They must begin, though, by cultivating a culture in the church where there is true gospel community and where members are open and comfortable speaking to one another about sin: a culture marked more by encouragement than correction. When we lead our church members to pray for and care for one another, we will be able to practice correction in a context of love. Does your church have such a healthy culture? What would it take to establish one?

A Better Authority

Truth be told, we all deserve judgment. But because Jesus received God's judgment on the cross on behalf of all repentant sinners, those who conquer by holding fast to Jesus and his teaching will not face it for themselves (Revelation 2 v 11; 20 v 6). Instead, in an echo of the language of Psalm 2 v 9, all who conquer will rule or judge the nations "with a rod of iron, as when earthen pots are broken in pieces, even as I myself have received authority from my Father" (Revelation 2 v 27).

Christian, this is your identity as a royal son or daughter. We are not to boast about our identity—we have only received it because we have received Jesus, who is "the morning star" (v 28; 22 v 16). Ironically, Jesus' rule and authority was prophesied by Balaam when he said, "I see him, but not now; I behold him, but not near; a star shall come out of Jacob, and a scepter shall rise out of Israel; it shall crush the forehead of Moab and break down all the sons of Sheth" (Numbers 24 v 17-19). Because we are united with Christ, we share in his rule. This is not just a message to the church in Thyatira; again, it's a message to all the churches—to all who have ears to hear what the Spirit says to the churches (Revelation 2 v 29).

I wish I'd listened sooner. Truth be told, early in my ministry I was a coward. I cared more about what people thought of me than doing and saying the necessary hard things in love. While I gained a reputation for being a "nice guy" because I always got along with everyone, the truth is, I was not nice at all. I was only loving myself. Ultimately, it's a love of self that keeps us from speaking the truth in love. It's a love of self that allows us to tolerate sin, rebellion, and even false teachers in the church.

If we're to overcome the danger of tolerance, we must first remember that Jesus is the Son to whom the Father has given all authority to judge—and his judgment is severe, thorough, just, and God-glorifying.

Then, if we truly love our brothers and sisters in Christ as God has loved us, we will exercise the biblical authority we share with Christ and confront unrepentant sin with patience, mercy, and grace. Discipline should never feel easy. Pragmatism will always argue against it. Yet it is better for our unrepentant brothers and sisters to fall under our judgment, than to fall under Jesus' final judgment. It takes real grace and wisdom to hold truth and love together so that you can help one another grow in Christ-likeness and escape Jesus' everlasting judgment—and may God give it to you.

¹ And to the angel of the church in Sardis write: "The words of him who has the seven spirits of God and the seven stars.

"I know your works. You have the reputation of being alive, but you are dead. ² Wake up, and strengthen what remains and is about to die, for I have not found your works complete in the sight of my God. ³ Remember, then, what you received and heard. Keep it, and repent. If you will not wake up, I will come like a thief, and you will not know at what hour I will come against you. ⁴ Yet you have still a few names in Sardis, people who have not soiled their garments, and they will walk with me in white, for they are worthy. ⁵ The one who conquers will be clothed thus in white garments, and I will never blot his name out of the book of life. I will confess his name before my Father and before his angels. ⁶ He who has an ear, let him hear what the Spirit says to the churches."

Revelation 3 v 1-6

A GOOD REPUTATION

What do you want visitors to say about your church?

As a pastor, it's a question that's on my mind. I'm sure church members also share a concern for their church's name in the community. One prominent church in our town is known as the "children's ministry church." If you want your kids to be served and have a great experience at church, that's the church for you. Another church is the "come as you are" church, where their slogan declares, "No perfect people allowed." These churches have worked hard to gain these reputations. But other churches gain a name by default. Since we live in a university city, we have the "college church" that attracts many students and young singles. We have "traditional" and "contemporary" churches, "charismatic" and "anti-charismatic" churches, "denominational" and "non-denominational" churches. Potential visitors will even tend to make decisions about a church based on its name—

"First Baptist Church" gives off a distinctly different vibe than "New Spring Community."

When I greet visitors at my church, High Pointe, I like to ask them a few questions: "Have you visited with us before? How did you hear about us? What encouraged you about our service today?" Being committed to biblical exposition, I'm always particularly proud when they mention our reputation for sound preaching as what drew them to us. "We're looking for a real gospel-centered church, so yours is the first we've tried out." "Friends told us the teaching here was great, so we thought we'd come along." That's precisely the reputation I want High Pointe to have—and I start to feel smug that we've gained it.

But then the Holy Spirit convicts me and reminds me that pride, whether it's about our children's ministry or our theology, is sinful and opposed by God. And if we're not careful, our boasting in our convictions may gain us a reputation for being "alive" when in fact, we're just another church offering what a certain consumer wants: in our case, reformed theology.

The problem, however, is that when all is said and done, it doesn't matter how visitors to your town may assess your church. Jesus' assessment is the only one that matters. The real question is: how does *Jesus* evaluate your church? That's the question answered in the message to the church at Sardis.

What this church and your church face is the danger of pride: that we would rely on our own ability to build the church and boast in the name we've made for ourselves, when in fact, underneath the exterior, Jesus says that we're "dead."

The True Source of Church Life
It's a dangerous thing to take our eyes off Jesus and make much of ourselves. So, as with every other church, Jesus

calls the church in Sardis back to the vision of himself from Revelation 1 v 9-20. He reminds them that he alone "has the seven spirits of God and the seven stars" (3 v 1a).

"Seven spirits of God?!" you might wonder. Remember, throughout this prophetic letter, numbers are used symbolically. Multiples of seven and ten communicate fullness: seven, fullness of quality; ten, fullness of quantity. So in 1 v 4-5, John greets the seven churches of Asia Minor with grace from the triune God: the Father, "him who is and who was and who is to come"; the Son, "Jesus Christ"; and the Holy Spirit, "the seven spirits who are before his throne." Here the "seven spirits" of God symbolize the Holy Spirit in his fullness, the source of life. Now in 3 v 1 we're told that Jesus possesses the Spirit and "the seven stars," which we know from 1 v 20 are "the angels of the seven churches." These angels represent the churches before the throne and speak Jesus' words to the churches. By declaring that he holds them in his right hand (1 v 16), Jesus not only reveals his sovereignty over the churches and their messengers; he also reveals that he is the source of the messages to the churches.

When we put this picture together, we're meant to see that Jesus alone gives life to the church by his Spirit and his word—so there is absolutely no room for human pride.

What's in a Name?

Why would the church in Sardis have needed to see this aspect of the risen Christ? Because they were proud! They trusted in their "reputation of being alive." The word translated "reputation" in verse 1b, is literally "name." And throughout this message, Jesus emphasizes the concept of "name" (here, and in verse 4 and twice in verse 5).

Why might a church gain a "name" for being "alive"? We may be tempted to think our church is "alive" when attendance is high and growing: lots of young people, both single and married, are present; the nursery is overflowing; and the budget is increasing. Perhaps you're part of a generation that connected "life" in a church with activity. To you, a church is "alive" when the calendar is filled with ministries, programs, Bible studies, home groups, outreach, and discipleship. Or maybe you're from the generation that sees "life" in the church when it's busy in the community: partnering with public schools, helping the poor, feeding the hungry, and seeking to end human trafficking. In the United States, at least, some want to be a part of a church that is "alive" in influence. Older evangelicals tend to push for influence in the political arena, while younger evangelicals are often more concerned with social justice.

For some, the church that is "alive" is the "relevant" church—the church with a seamless website, the "come as you are" ambience, and a stupendous coffee bar. Now, those who are "spiritual" laugh at that because they know that "life" in a church is evident in the liveliness of the music, the repetition of the lyrics, the lifting of hands, the candles, the incense, or the mood lighting. But let's not forget about the "super-spiritual." They see "life" in a church's doctrinal purity and Spirit-filled preaching. There are lots of reasons why we may be confident that our church is alive—not like *those other ones*. And whether consciously or subconsciously, we're all trying to build our church's "brand."

Don't get me wrong. It's right to want to see our churches grow; to want to see unbelieving people profess faith in Christ and be incorporated into the church. We want to grow in our generosity to advance the gospel. We want to see our members serve in the church and in the community. We want to influence the world with the gospel. We want our corporate worship to be Christ-exalting and Spirit-filled. We want to have right doctrine. These good desires are not the problem. The problem is trusting in these things to give us life, or trusting that we are "alive" as a church just because we're doing them. We need to be careful how we assess churches, including our own.

The church in Sardis had a "name" for being "alive." If you had moved to Sardis toward the end of the first century, and you had asked for church recommendations, everyone would have said, "You must check out the church in Sardis—that place is alive. There's no other church like it around." Jesus, however, knows their "works"—and from his perspective, they're not really "alive" but "dead" (3 v 1-2). You can have a full program and be dead. You can have full pews and be dead. The Christians in Sardis were deceived.

Sadly, the church in Sardis mirrored their city's history. Sardis boasted of two things: their wealth and their natural defenses. The city was situated on the top of a hill, surrounded by cliffs that were thought to be unscalable. So confident were they in their natural defenses that they failed to put guards at the most dangerous precipice. But their arrogance led to their defeat, not once, but twice. At the most dangerous point, where they least expected it, daring warriors risked their lives to take the city by surprise. In addition, a great earthquake in AD 17 destroyed Sardis, leaving it with great debt. The Sardians, once proud of their wealth and natural defenses, were defeated. Theirs is a real riches-to-rags story—they were caught off guard and destroyed. That's the danger of pride!

The Christians in Sardis are not alone in their pride, are they? Today, we too are prone to trust in our own power and ability to build Christ's church—and to boast in the reputation we've built for ourselves rather than boast in Christ. If we're to overcome this danger, we too must first look to the risen Christ, who alone builds his church by his word and Spirit. In him is life. And that's exactly what we witness throughout Acts. The church comes to life as Jesus' word goes out and is attended by his Spirit, so that "the word of God continued to increase" as the church grew (Acts 6 v 7).

But take heart. If you've got a church that looks good on the outside, but underneath is proud or dead or both, Jesus has a resuscitation plan.

How to Restore Life by Killing Pride

In a string of five commands, Jesus shows the church in Sardis what they must do to stave off their imminent death. If we're to overcome the danger of pride, we need to heed these same warnings.

1. Wake Up!

Like the city of Sardis, the church trusted in its "name" and let down its guard. Now Jesus calls them to constantly be awake, vigilant, alert (Revelation 3 v 2a). We find this same command throughout the New Testament. Jesus commanded his disciples to "stay awake, for you do not know on what day your Lord is coming" (Matthew 24 v 42). In the Garden of Gethsemane, Jesus asked Peter, James, and John to stay awake with him while he prayed. They fell asleep, so Jesus charged them to "watch and pray that you may not enter into temptation" (26 v 38-41). And in Revelation 16 v 15, as the climax of Jesus' judgment is approaching at the battle of Armageddon, Jesus warns, "Behold, I am coming like a thief! Blessed is the one who stays awake, keeping his garments on, that he may not go about naked and be seen exposed."

The New Testament warnings to "stay awake" remind us to look for the return of Christ, for he will come "like a thief," and we don't want to be caught off guard, sleeping on the job. And the history of Sardis should remind us of our need to "wake up" to enemy attacks of the devil's temptations. In what ways have we, like the city of Sardis, let down our guard? Are we living as if Christ could come at any moment? Wake up!

2. Strengthen What Is about to Die

Jesus' assessment of the church in Sardis is stark at first, but he offers hope. *Take heart! You're not dead yet*—there is something there that is "about to die" but can still be revived (3 v 2). Let this be a caution to those of us who tend to be hypercritical and are quick to label churches as "dead." No church appears as dead as the one in Sardis by Jesus' estimation, but there is still enough in the church that can be strengthened. If you're a Christian who finds yourself in a church that appears dead, let this truth give you hope.

The church appears "dead" because their works are lacking. Jesus "knows their works" (v 1), but they are "not ... complete" (v 2). To be sure, we are not saved by our works, but if we are saved, our faith will produce works. As James says, "Faith by itself, if it does not have works, is dead" (James 2 v 14-17), and this seems to be the case with the church in Sardis. So, they must strengthen what is about to die—their faith must give evidence of salvation through good deeds.

After all, at the final judgment, Jesus "will give to each of you according to your works" (Revelation 2 v 23).

What works is Jesus talking about? Clearly, the church in Sardis must have been doing *something* to have gained a reputation for being alive (3 v 1). But frenetic activity is not the same as good works motivated by faith—it's *what* you're doing and *why* that matters, not just the fact that you're *doing* something. Jesus commended the Ephesian Christians for their works of toil, patient endurance, and fighting for doctrinal purity (2 v 2); he commended the Thyatirans for their works of "love and faith and service and patient endurance" (2 v 19). Essentially, Jesus exposes that the church in Sardis is lacking in the "good works, which God prepared beforehand, that we should walk in them" (Ephesians 2 v 10). Consequently, Jesus commands them to grow in good works.

This command warrants a warning, however. It is possible for a church to call for good works apart from the gospel and the power of the Holy Spirit. This is a danger for the culturally "conservative" church today. This is the church that doesn't say much about the gospel, but says a lot about alcohol, dancing, playing cards, and other worldly entertainments. Well, it only says one thing—*no!* In this church there is no gospel appeal because there is no gospel proclamation. They simply tell you that in order to come to Christ you must clean up your act. In fact, in order just to come to church, you'd better clean up your act. This is a message from the pit of hell. The gospel reminds us that we are powerless to clean up our own act. That is why we need Jesus to give us life by his word and his Spirit—and he offers life to all who come to him in repentance and faith just as they are. And when you do, he is the One who promises to clean you up (Ephesians 5 v 25-27).

This is indeed *good news*—this is the gospel! When we believe this gospel, it will produce the fruit of good works. That's what Jesus says next...

3 & 4. Remember the Gospel and Keep It

These two commands belong together and show us how to stay awake and strengthen what remains (Revelation 3 v 3). The Sardians' slumber and incomplete works were evidence that they had forgotten the gospel; as a result, they were not keeping it. We forget the gospel when we assume it. We need the gospel not only for new spiritual life; we need it for ongoing spiritual life. And yet, it's so easy to assume that our church knows and understands it. We might leave the gospel reminder out of a sermon because we assume people will be able to "fill in the gap" and we want to have time to say something "meatier" instead. We might skip some questions in a Bible study because the answers seem so obvious.

But the theologian Don Carson reminds us that the gospel may be lost in just one generation. The first generation *believes* the gospel and faithfully applies all its implications to their personal, church, and public life. The second generation *assumes* the gospel, but continues to advance and apply its implications. The third generation *denies* the gospel, and embraces only its implications. Consider the trajectory of Protestant liberal churches. Though they originated with a strong gospel foundation, today they are known for their clothes closets, food pantries, and hospitals. Their mission trips entail building homes and church buildings, but not the church of Jesus Christ through gospel proclamation. However alive your church looks now, it too is only a couple of generations away from potential death.

Jesus commands the church in Sardis to "remember, then, what you received and heard" (Revelation 3 v 3). Paul uses the same language with the Corinthians when he charges them, "Now I would remind you, brothers, of the gospel I preached to you, which you received, in which you stand, and by which you are being saved, if you hold fast to the word I preached to you" (1 Corinthians 15 v 1-2). The gospel is the revelation of God about Jesus: the good news that though we deserve God's judgment, God has offered Jesus to live the life God requires of us and pay the penalty of sin we owe. And whoever embraces God's offer, through repentance and faith, receives forgiveness of sin and a right standing before God. In the mystery of God's sovereign grace, new life comes about when the gospel word is preached and is attended by the Holy Spirit. As Peter declares, "You have been born again, not of perishable seed but of imperishable, through the living and abiding word of God" (1 Peter 1 v 23). This is what the Sardian Christians had received and heard.

But the Christian life is not merely about "hearing" a gospel word and agreeing with it. One sign of genuine faith is obedience—"keeping" the gospel (Revelation 3 v 3). In the Great Commission, Jesus commands his disciples, not simply to make converts or to lead people to decisions for Christ. He commissions us to announce the gospel to all peoples; to incorporate into the church through baptism those who respond with repentance and faith; and to teach them to "keep" all Jesus has commanded (Matthew 28 v 19-20, the same word as in Revelation 3 v 3). This all-encompassing gospel message is the foundation of the church; it is the basis on which Jesus is building his church. Consequently, there is no other foundation upon which we may build Jesus' church: not feelings, not numbers, not activity, not ministries, not music, not relevance, not coffee, but Christ and Christ alone. All these things can adorn the gospel, but they are not its content.

As we keep the gospel, it should affect every area of our lives, individually and as a church. Consider the "name" we Christians have in our culture. Our reputation is not positive in many instances. But when we genuinely keep the gospel, we will serve this unbelieving, hostile world as faithful ambassadors of King Jesus. The opposite of a proud Christian is a grateful one—one who's grateful for what Jesus has done for them when they know they didn't deserve it. If we keep the gospel we'll be motivated by the power of the Spirit instead of the passions of the world. Our lives will be marked by the works of the Spirit instead of the works of the flesh (Galatians 5 v 16-24). We'll be more concerned with making Jesus look good than trying to make ourselves look good. We'll serve our neighbors instead of serving our own interests and desires. We'll seek to build up other people rather than trying to build our own little kingdoms. Wouldn't our reputation in our community change for the better if we started living consistently with the gospel of Jesus Christ?

Imagine the impact that keeping the gospel would have on the life of a church too. If we were to walk together according to this glorious gospel, we would fight to maintain the unity of the Spirit instead of fighting one another to get our own way. Imagine how different committee meetings might be or how members' meetings would change if, rather than fighting for our preferences, we deferred to one another on issues where there is room for disagreement—putting ourselves out for others because that's what Jesus did for us. Think about how the culture of our church would change when, rather than assuming the worst of someone, we started assuming the best because they're a brother or sister for whom Christ died. Imagine relationships where it's safe to speak the truth of the gospel to one another, both encouraging and correcting in love; where it's safe to confess sin and grant forgiveness—because we know we have our Father's forgiveness already. Such a church would gain a reputation for being alive!

But keeping the gospel does not happen naturally. We must be vigilant; we must remain awake! So pastors must preach this gospel faithfully and regularly each Sunday. And this gospel must be faithfully received by the church and reverberate throughout the homes of the congregation: at the dinner table, the family room, our children's bedrooms. And we must speak this gospel throughout the life of the church. Our curriculum, from children to senior adults, from small groups to Sunday-school classes, should communicate and clarify this gospel in order to equip us to live lives worthy of it. Only by such diligence will we stay awake, strengthen what is dying, and remember and keep the gospel.

Chances are though, that your church doesn't match the picture I've just described. So what must we do if we have in any way forgotten the gospel?

5. Repent

If we've assumed, forgotten, or even rejected the gospel, Jesus calls us to repent: to change our thinking about Christ and the source of true life in the church (Revelation 3 v 3). We must stop thinking we can produce "life" in the church by our own strength, creativity, and programming. Instead of pride, we should cultivate humility. Rather than boast, we should give thanks for the life we do have in Christ by his word and Spirit. But, if we don't repent, Jesus warns that he "will come like a thief, and you will not know at what hour I will come against you." If we continue in our gospel slumber, Jesus will come in judgment, and we will be caught off guard, just like the Sardians.

Peter reminds us that judgment begins with the church (1 Peter 4 v 17). More than likely, Jesus is not speaking about final judgment here, but of a visitation of judgment upon the church in Sardis in which he removes their lampstand. Sometimes Jesus' judgment appears slow in coming, but we must remember that it will come. The good news is that while the call to repentance still stands, we have hope. No matter how sick our church may be, Christ can bring it to life through the gospel.

A Faithful Few

Jesus only had "a few things against" the church in Pergamum (Revelation 2 v 14). Sadly, Jesus has much against the church in Sardis. And yet, there are "still a few names in Sardis, people who have not soiled their garments" (3 v 4a). So long as there are a few names in our churches who are faithful, we can strengthen what remains. To those who remain faithful, Jesus says, "They will walk with me in white, for they are worthy" (v 4). Again, it's not that they have earned God's favor; it's that they have remembered the gospel they heard and kept it, their holiness giving evidence of their genuine faith. The imagery of walking with Jesus in white garments likely points to the idea that the Romans would celebrate military victories in a procession, wearing white robes. So, while Sardis was sacked twice because they let down their guard, and while the church in Sardis must wake up lest it be sacked by Christ, the "one who conquers will be clothed thus in white garments"—they will be victors marching with King Jesus (v 5).

Note also the second promise. Instead of judgment, the one who conquers by remembering the gospel and keeping it will receive eternal life: Jesus "will never blot his name out of the book of life." This does not mean we can lose our salvation (v 5). It is a threat, much like in Matthew 7 v 21-23, that those who do not remain faithful and therefore prove that they are not Christians because they don't keep the gospel, will be judged according to their works. But, those who are faithful should see this promise as an assurance that Jesus, who gave them life by his word and Spirit, will ensure they persevere to the end. If we remember the gospel and keep it, we have no reason to fear that our name will ever be blotted out of the book of life.

Finally, those who conquer by remembering the gospel and keeping it will receive the only name recognition that matters. Jesus declares, "I will confess his name before my Father and before his angels" (Revelation 3 v 5). While we try so hard to make much of ourselves and our churches before the world, the only name recognition we should long for is our Lord's. Let his assessment of you be enough for you.

A church can have a good name in the community for any number of reasons. But pray that your church would be known not for your size or budget or buildings, not for your community impact or political influence, not for your music style or band, not for your website or coffee, not even for having the right doctrine or great preaching—but for the fact that you cling to Christ, remember his gospel, and keep his word. Too many churches have chased name recognition but not cherished the gospel. Sadly, some of those churches no longer exist, and the buildings they met in are now mosques, or community centers, or housing.

When the risen Christ assesses your church, what will he say? If your life together as a church is rooted and grounded in the life-giving gospel and the life-giving Spirit, then regardless of what label the world may slap on you, Jesus will declare, *The world may call you dead, but you are alive!*

DANGER SIX
SELF-DOUBT

"*⁷ And to the angel of the church in Philadelphia write: "The words of the holy one, the true one, who has the key of David, who opens and no one will shut, who shuts and no one opens.*

⁸ "I know your works. Behold, I have set before you an open door, which no one is able to shut. I know that you have but little power, and yet you have kept my word and have not denied my name. ⁹ Behold, I will make those of the synagogue of Satan who say that they are Jews and are not, but lie—behold, I will make them come and bow down before your feet, and they will learn that I have loved you. ¹⁰ Because you have kept my word about patient endurance, I will keep you from the hour of trial that is coming on the whole world, to try those who dwell on the earth. ¹¹ I am coming soon. Hold fast what you have, so that no one may seize your crown. ¹² The one who conquers, I will make him a pillar in the temple of my God. Never shall he go out of it, and I will write on him the name of my God, and the name of the city of my God, the new Jerusalem, which comes down from my God out of heaven, and my own new name. ¹³ He who has an ear, let him hear what the Spirit says to the churches."

Revelation 3 v 7-13

Church, we have a problem.

OK, so we have more than one problem. But for some time now, Christians in the West have bought into the notion that mega-churches, with their celebrity pastors, are the best, most successful, and most influential ministries around, and that they are what all churches should strive to become. The problem is two-fold. We create the celebrity pastors and mega-churches by consuming their sermons and resources, and they (some of them, but by no means all of them) appear convinced that the kingdom cannot go on without them. Consequently, believing themselves to be God's gift to the kingdom, these churches reproduce themselves on multiple campuses and project their talking-head pastors on video screens. It's as if they're saying, "Since those little churches are no longer relevant or creative enough to reach the younger generations, it's up to us."

Admittedly, I'm painting with a broad brush. Many of the "celebrity" pastors I know work hard to distance themselves from such a status. They are humble brothers who seek to faithfully shepherd all the theological consumers that enter their church's doors. And there's nothing inherently wrong with being a large church. The first church in Acts was a mega-church. Still, because we Western Christians are also so prone to consumerism, all an entrepreneurial pastor has to do to become successful is to meet our "felt needs," whether those felt needs are practical or theological. As a result, these "successful" pastors and churches are rewarded with numerical growth, cultural influence, and denominational or network recognition. And if we're not careful, we will assume that their ministry "success" equals God's blessing, and that our lack of ministry "success" equals God's rejection.

As someone whose first pastorate was of a church of just over 100 members, I know what it's like to feel irrelevant—even a failure—in comparison to larger churches with ample resources and big-name pastors. Although of course in some settings a church of 100 sounds like a thriving success story! It's all relative. Either way, the reminders of our church's lack of "success" are ever before us: the young family that leaves for a larger, programmatic church; the pastors' conference that fills its plenaries with "famed" pastors; the denomination or network that rewards the "successful" churches at its annual gathering; or the Christian publisher who will only ever consider publishing books by celebrity pastors or authors with platforms.

Some of us see the allure of celebrity status and mega-church size, and respond like the church in Sardis from the last chapter—busily trying to produce "success" in our own strength. But in this message, Jesus exposes an opposite yet equally dangerous response. When we wrongly equate apparent "success" in ministry with God's blessing, we "normal" pastors and "regular" Christians can become dejected by the seeming lack of success of our church. We interpret our apparent failure in ministry to mean God's hand is not upon us. We easily grow bitter and start grumbling. We find ourselves seeing other churches as rivals, not as gospel partners. If we're a church member, we might begin to wish we had a different pastor or move to a different church with more to offer. If we're a church leader, we may even become so discouraged that we're tempted to leave the ministry, abandon our church, or worse yet, doubt our own standing before God. That's the danger of self-doubt. And that's the danger facing the church in Philadelphia in Revelation 3 v 7-13.

Holy, True Key-Holder

Where do you turn when you're despondent and filled with self-doubt—about your church, your ministry, or even your standing before God? There's only one place worth looking: to the risen Christ. He alone is "the holy one, the true one" (v 7). The Jews in the Old Testament awaited a king from David's line whom God would anoint with his Spirit to lead his people out of exile and restore the kingdom to Israel. Jesus is this "true" Messiah of God! He has been given "the key of David"—he alone has authority over David's eternal kingdom, the new Jerusalem, deciding who may enter in. If Jesus opens the door of the new Jerusalem to anyone, no one else may shut it. Likewise, if Jesus shuts the door of the new Jerusalem to any one, no one else may open it.

The Jews in first-century Philadelphia believed themselves to be the true people of God because they were Jews: that is, Abraham's biological offspring. They rejected Jesus as the true Messiah and made out that the door of the eternal kingdom was shut in the Christians' faces because they could not, after all, be the true people of God. In all likelihood, their repeated rejection by the Jews would eventually lead the Christians in Philadelphia to doubt themselves: did they really have a place in the heavenly new Jerusalem, or had they got it all horribly wrong?

An Open Door

But Jesus knows his people, and he knows their works. Since he alone has the key of David, he had opened the door of the new Jerusalem to the Christians in Philadelphia—and the Jews could not shut it (v 8). Jesus opens or shuts the door of the kingdom to individuals based on their response to him, not on their Jewish ethnicity. All who recognize Jesus as the true Messiah may enter in, whether Jew or Gentile, male or female, black or white, Asian or Hispanic.

This is so important to remember when we're tempted to doubt our standing before God or question the purpose of our ministry. We need to fix our eyes on the risen Christ and remember that he alone determines who's in and who's out based on our response to him. If you have embraced Jesus as the One who saves his people, he has opened the door of the kingdom to you. No one may shut it.

Sadly, too many professing Christians try to shut the door of the kingdom to other followers of Christ. Perhaps you're a new Christian, and someone tells you that you cannot be a true Christian unless you experience a "second blessing" or "baptism in the Spirit." Maybe you're a young church and a group of believers joins you and they start saying that you cannot be a true Christian unless you homeschool your children. These "superior" Christians may offer any number of things that you must do or believe to be a "real" Christian: a specific view of the age of the earth, the spiritual gifts, the five points of Calvinism, the five points of Arminianism, or particular convictions on alcohol or tattoos or smoking or entertainment or the Sabbath or the Lord's Day... Essentially, what they are doing is "shutting" the door of the kingdom to those who differ from them in their beliefs. Don't listen to them! Jesus plus anything equals heresy. We can't add anything to the work that Jesus has done on our behalf. If you've trusted in Christ, he has opened the door of the kingdom to you; no one can shut you out.

If rejection by the Jews wasn't enough, the church in Philadelphia also had "but little power." They were small, weak, and powerless. They had little influence in their world. "And yet," declares Jesus, "you have kept my word and have not denied my name" (v 8). While the church in Philadelphia may not have been the mega-church of Jerusalem or had "celebrity" pastors like Peter, James, and John, they remained faithful in the face of persecution. Contrary to what evangelicals may be tempted to believe today, bigger is not always better or more faithful. What pleases Jesus is not the size of our congregation or the numbers in our budget or the breadth of our influence; what pleases Jesus is faithfulness. And this is good news for thousands of churches who identify with the Philadelphian Christians.

In the United States at least, most churches are more like the one in Philadelphia than the one in Jerusalem. I pastored one such church in a rural setting, surrounded by corn and cattle. The town itself did not experience much population growth, so there was no influx of new believers looking for churches. In a situation like that it's easy for both pastor and people to become discouraged when you don't witness many conversions, when there is no dramatic growth in numbers, when the budget is the same year after year, and when the church has little influence in the community.

Yet at the same time, there was one church across town that *was* growing. They offered the best children's and youth ministry; they catered to the "felt needs" of the people; they creatively used the latest technologies in their services. But because the population of our town was static, their growth came at the expense of many of the other churches in the area. When you lose families in your church to that, it's easy to be discouraged, dejected, and discontent. It became easy to wonder if we were doing enough as a church or if I was a failure as a pastor. After all, if we simply preached and lived out the word, wouldn't God bless us? And if God wasn't blessing us, was he rejecting us?

When we compare our church to other "successful" churches and, if we're pastors, ourselves to other "famous" pastors, it's easy to become discouraged and believe the lie that we're somehow deficient, and that God is not pleased with us. When this happens, we begin to duck out of active ministry: pastors leave and elders resign. Or we lose joy: we start to resent the time we're spending in ministry, or we get annoyed at what other people are or aren't doing. We might try to fix things by moving to a bigger church, or leave church altogether. And if someone gives up on church, then all too often it's not long before they give up on Jesus.

But we need this message to the church in Philadelphia because it reminds us that our status as Christians is firm with Jesus, and that he is pleased with faithfulness, not outward "success." Jesus is the one who can open and shut the door, so he's the one who is responsible for the church's growth. We are called to be faithful—only Jesus can make us fruitful. In some seasons he does and in some seasons he doesn't; but both seasons call for humble confidence in Christ.

I now have the privilege of pastoring a church that is larger than the average church in the United States. We have multiple staff members and a growing budget. Yet the challenge today is the same as it was when I pastored a church of just over 100—to remain faithful. But I have to confess, I have it easier than most pastors. My heroes in the faith are bi-vocational pastors: those brothers who pastor churches so small that they cannot afford to pay their pastors.

These brothers normally work a full-time job, while also fulfilling all the responsibilities of a full-time pastor: sermon preparation, hospital visitation, pastoral care. These faithful brothers will likely never be a plenary speaker at The Gospel Coalition Conference or Together for the Gospel; they will likely never experience massive growth and be recognized by their denomination or network; and they will likely never be pursued by a Christian publisher for a book deal—but they are faithful. Week in and week out, they keep Jesus' word and do not deny him, and they lead their churches to pursue that same faithfulness.

Or I think of women who labor long hours in the service of their church, fitting it round employment or home responsibilities. They likely won't be asked to headline a national women's conference or to sign a book deal either, but they too are faithful and keep Jesus' word. It is believers like these and faithful churches like the ones they serve who, along with the church in Philadelphia, will be vindicated by the risen Christ at the last day.

A Better Day Is Coming

"How long until we start to see some growth?" "How long before God raises up the leaders we need?" "Will this ever get any easier?" "Am I just not cut out for this?" If you're asking these kinds of questions, you're in good company. What you need to hear is the same thing the church in Philadelphia needed to hear: Jesus' promises guaranteeing vindication, affirmation, and security in the new Jerusalem.

Vindication

The Jews looked forward to the restoration of Israel at the hands of an anointed king from David's line, based on a new covenant. Isaiah even announced that the glory of this future kingdom would draw all the nations and kings to this new Jerusalem (Isaiah 60 v 3-4). Isaiah prophesied that Israel's enemies, who had afflicted them, "shall come bending low to you, and all who despised you shall bow down at your feet; they shall call you the City of the LORD, the Zion of the Holy One of Israel" (v 14). For a beleaguered people in exile in a foreign land, this was a powerful message of hope.

But now, in a great reversal, Jesus charges that when the Jews call themselves the true people of God, they are lying. They aren't the people of God at all. Why? Because they have rejected "the holy [and] true one" with the real power to open and shut the door to the eternal kingdom (Revelation 3 v 7). In addition, because they oppose the Philadelphian

Christians, who really are the true people of God, the Jews are "the synagogue of Satan." Jesus will vindicate his true people, the church, by causing the Jews to "come and bow down before your feet, and they will learn that I have loved you" (v 9). In saying these things, Jesus turns Isaiah 60 v 14 on its head—Jesus applies this promise of vindication not to the Jews, but to the church. It's the Jews, and anyone who has rejected Jesus, who will come crawling.

And on that final day of God's judgment, all who embrace Jesus Christ will be vindicated. We will be shown to be God's true people, and God will declare, "I have loved you." Therefore, if we have come to Christ, we have no reason to doubt our standing before God. Our acceptance before God is not based on the size of our faith or the size of our ministries; it is based solely on the substitutionary life, death, and resurrection of Jesus, by which he inaugurated the new covenant and established the true people of God. So, don't look for vindication in the size of your church or the breadth of your influence or the status people give you; look to the risen Christ and rest in the status he has gained for you.

Affirmation

The church in Philadelphia looks weak in the world's eyes. They aren't going to win any awards any time soon. But Jesus says that they already have a prize that is immeasurably better: a crown. This image would remind the Philadelphians of the award victorious athletes would receive. It's an award that we don't need to strive to win for ourselves, because Jesus has won it for us. When God looks at us, he is pleased with us. He doesn't see our sin or our weaknesses or our failures—he sees Christ's victory on our behalf.

And this affirmation is all that counts in the final judgment. Jesus promises that for all those who remain faithful and keep his "word about patient endurance," Jesus himself "will keep [them] from the hour of trial that is coming on the whole world" (v 10). Final judgment is coming on all those who "dwell on the earth"—all who reject Christ, whether Jew or Gentile. For those whose citizenship is already in heaven, our sin has already been judged in Jesus—so we will be "kept from" this final judgment. Until then, Jesus promises to be with us in our struggles and suffering, and to see us through.

All we have to do is to cling on to Jesus. He reminds us to "hold fast what you have"—that is Christ and the gospel—"so that no one may seize your crown" (v 11). Once again, Jesus reminds us that what pleases him is faithfulness: holding fast—not the size of our church, not the reputation of our church, and most definitely not the fame of our pastor. So while the world is busy giving away awards and recognition, remember that Jesus is coming soon and is bringing a better prize—a crown of victory that no one can take away from us.

Eternal Security

Finally, and most comforting to the doubting Philadelphians, Jesus promises eternal security in the new Jerusalem. Jesus promises to make every conqueror "a pillar in the temple of my God" (v 12). Imagine living in a city like Philadelphia, where earthquakes were common. Every time there is an earthquake, you have to evacuate your home. And imagine returning to the city to find the temples and their pillars crumbling and destroyed. Against this backdrop, Jesus offers an image of permanence. In effect, he promises: *If I've opened the door to you and you persevere, if you hold fast, not only will you receive a crown, but you have eternal security. You will be a pillar in the temple of my God and you will never have to go out of there. You will enjoy his love forever. You will never have to evacuate from the presence of God.*

And in God's presence, Jesus promises intimate fellowship with God. By writing on us "the name of my God," Jesus reminds us that we belong to God, that we have his name (v 12). My children have my name: Sanchez. Maybe your children have your name. But for those who are in Christ, they will have God's name. As those who belong to God, we are promised intimate fellowship with him in his presence— far more love and security than you find in even the closest-knit family.

We'll also have "the name of the city of [our] God." The fact that we will have the name of the new Jerusalem points to our heavenly citizenship. That's why we're contrasted with the earth-dwellers. All who belong to Christ are promised citizenship in the heavenly Jerusalem. We will have eternal security and permanent intimate fellowship with the one true, holy God of all things. Like the Philadelphians, you may feel rejected; you may feel alone; you may feel unimportant, discouraged, and even doubtful about your salvation. This message is meant to encourage you, to relieve your doubt, and to communicate to you the permanence and eternal security of salvation in Christ—a salvation that cannot be taken away. That's good news for all Christians everywhere. "He who has an ear, let him hear what the Spirit says to the churches" (v 13).

In 1850, at the age of 15, a not-yet-converted Charles Spurgeon was on his way to his regular church, when a snowstorm forced him to find shelter in a small Primitive Methodist church on Artillery Street in Colchester, England. The pastor of this church was himself kept from attending due to the storm, so a lay preacher got up and began to preach Isaiah 45 v 22: "Look unto me, and be ye saved, all the ends of the earth" (KJV). Not being a man of great oratorical skill, the lay preacher repeated the text over and over again, and then turned to Spurgeon and spoke directly to him, pleading with him: "Young man, look to Jesus Christ." As Spurgeon recounted the events of that evening, he said, "There and then the cloud was gone, the darkness had rolled away, and that moment I saw the sun; and I could have risen that moment and sung with the most enthusiastic of them of the Precious Blood of Christ."

Spurgeon would go on to become one of the greatest preachers of all time, preaching to large crowds in various venues. Known as "the Prince of Preachers," Spurgeon was what we might now call a celebrity pastor, leading the mega-church of his day. I thank God for Charles Spurgeon. He is a model for us today—not for his apparent ministry "successes," but for his faithfulness. Spurgeon also reminds us that we do not have to pit faithfulness and fruitfulness against each other. He was both.

What I love about Spurgeon's conversion story, though, is that it reminds us that there are faithful "little" churches throughout the world that God may just use to raise up some of the most fruitful pastors of faithful churches in the future. Perhaps yours is one of them. Spurgeon's story reminds us that faithfulness and fruitfulness go hand in hand, but not always in the same church.

So whether God grants us fruitfulness or simply calls us to prepare the ground for those who will come after us, remember that God does not measure success as we do. But he does honor faithfulness—now, and in eternity—regardless of what the outward results may look like. So stay faithful, and you never know quite what God may be pleased to use you for.

DANGER SEVEN SELF SUFFICIENCY

¹⁴ And to the angel of the church in Laodicea write: "The words of the Amen, the faithful and true witness, the beginning of God's creation.

¹⁵ "I know your works: you are neither cold nor hot. Would that you were either cold or hot! ¹⁶ So, because you are lukewarm, and neither hot nor cold, I will spit you out of my mouth. ¹⁷ For you say, I am rich, I have prospered, and I need nothing, not realizing that you are wretched, pitiable, poor, blind, and naked. ¹⁸ I counsel you to buy from me gold refined by fire, so that you may be rich, and white garments so that you may clothe yourself and the shame of your nakedness may not be seen, and salve to anoint your eyes, so that you may see. ¹⁹ Those whom I love, I reprove and discipline, so be zealous and repent. ²⁰ Behold, I stand at the door and knock. If anyone hears my voice and opens the door, I will come in to him and eat with him, and he with me. ²¹ The one who conquers, I will grant him to sit with me on my throne, as I also conquered and sat down with my Father on his throne. ²² He who has an ear, let him hear what the Spirit says to the churches."

Revelation 3 v 14-22

SELF SUFFICIENCY

"The United States is the most dangerous place to raise your children."

My friend had just finished preaching as a guest at our church, challenging us to consider God's call to forsake comfort and take the gospel to difficult and dangerous places. After the sermon, we all wanted to go with him. The only problem was that he was on his way to pastor a fledgling church not too far from the heart of the Islamic State. One of our members shared a desire to go, but he clarified that his children were still small, and my friend was going to one of the most dangerous places in the world to raise a family. Without hesitation, my friend said, "The United States is the most dangerous place to raise your children."

For Christians, the most dangerous places to live are not where our safety may be compromised or where our lives may be at risk; the most dangerous places for Christians are where our souls are most at risk. And if there's one thing that strangles our faith more than anything else it's this: prosperity. Wealth is what makes Western culture spiritually fatal.

The problem is that affluence and prosperity so easily deceive us into believing we don't need anyone else: not even God. We don't need to pray, "Give us this day our daily bread" because the pantry is stocked full—not just of the necessary staple foods in our diets, but of Coca Cola, Doritos, and Hershey bars (unless, of course, you prefer Perrier, veggie chips, and organic dark chocolate). But prosperity has been a stumbling block for God's people throughout history: from the time God warned Israel about its dangers (Deuteronomy 31 v 19-20), to when Jesus warned his disciples not to store their treasures here on earth (Matthew 6 v 19-24), to the apostle Paul reminding Timothy that the love of money had led some away from the faith to much pain (1 Timothy 6 v 10). And Jesus' message to the church in Laodicea warns us of this same danger— the danger of self-sufficiency. When blessed with prosperity, as many of us in the developed world are, we must guard against the danger of becoming complacent in our affluence, relying on our own wealth and power, and becoming blind to our spiritual need. Instead, we must fight self-sufficiency by looking to the risen Christ and relying on him fully for everything we may need in this life.

Who We Really Need

In this last message, Jesus starts by pointing us not to the vision from Revelation 1, but to a vision, seemingly, from Isaiah 65. Here, God promises to judge those who reject him (65 v 11-12) and to restore his faithful people by creating "new heavens and a new earth" (v 17). These verses in Isaiah also echo God's promises to Abram (Genesis 12 v 1-3)—there's mention of blessings and land. And just as God changed Abram's name to Abraham as a symbol of his covenant with him (17 v 1-8), those who enter God's new creation will be those with a new name and who bless themselves by "the God of truth" (Isaiah 65 v 15-16). The word translated "truth" is the Hebrew word, "amen." In other words, those who enter into the blessing of the new creation are those who enter in by the God of the Amen.

That's why in Revelation 3 v 14, Jesus is "the Amen" of God. As the apostle Paul confirms in 2 Corinthians 1 v 20, "all the promises of God find their Yes in [Jesus]. That is why it is through him that we utter our Amen to God for his glory." When Jesus declares that he is "the Amen," he reminds the Laodicean Christians that he is God's confirmation of all the Abrahamic promises to bless the world and create a new heavens and a new earth. The fact that God has sent Christ into the world to bring about salvation confirms God's truthfulness concerning all his promises: *Amen, yes, I'll do it.* So, our hope is not in the wealth of this world; our hope is in the world to come that God has promised.

Jesus' second description of himself plays into a similar idea: Jesus is "the faithful and true witness" (Revelation 3 v 14). Because Jesus is God's Amen, God's truth, he is a witness to God's "trustworthy and true" promise that he will bring about a new creation for his people (Revelation 21 v 5)—a bit like a witness to a signature on a contract. That he is "faithful" carries with it connotations of suffering. Jesus not only confirmed God's promises; he faithfully fulfilled what was necessary so that those promises could come about.

Through his life, suffering, death, and resurrection, Jesus accomplished salvation so that all who come to him, God's Amen, receive the blessing of the new creation.

Finally, Jesus is the ruler over creation. That Jesus is "the beginning of God's creation" (2 v 14) does not mean he was the first created being. Jesus is God's Word, who already existed in "the beginning" (John 1 v 1-2). And in Revelation 21 v 6, God the Father, "the one who [is] seated on the throne," is "the Alpha and the Omega, the beginning and the end." Jesus too is "the Alpha and the Omega, the first and the last, the beginning and the end" (Revelation 22 v 13). The word translated "beginning" in verse 14 is also translated "ruler"—Jesus is the source, sustainer, and goal of creation. How foolish of us to ever think we don't need him! He provides for our every need; he sustains the universe, causing the sun to rise and the rain to fall, and the tide to come in only so far. And we await the day when he will bring about the new creation and bring God's people into it, just as God has promised.

This is the risen Christ who assesses the Laodicean church—and he's not about to pull any punches.

You Make Me Sick

You make me sick! Can you imagine Jesus saying that about your church, about you, about anyone?! It sounds so harsh—but that's what Jesus means when he tells the Laodiceans, "I will spit you out of my mouth" (3 v 16). The reason for this brutal assessment is that the prosperity the Laodicean Christians enjoy has made them self-sufficient. "For," Jesus charges them, "you say, I am rich, I have prospered, and I need nothing" (v 17). As a result of their prosperity, they are "lukewarm, and neither hot nor cold" (v 16). In other words, they are useless.

A little historical detail can help us better understand what Jesus is getting at here. The Laodiceans did not have drinkable water. The local water supply contained calcium carbonate which, when you drank it, made you vomit. As a result, they depended on nearby cities for drinkable water. Hieropolis had naturally hot water, but by the time it traveled to Laodicea via aqueducts, it was lukewarm—useless. Colossae had a cold-water supply, but by the time it traveled to Laodicea via aqueduct, it too was lukewarm—useless. Jesus captures Laodicea's water problem to expose their uselessness. He's not suggesting they be either "hot for Jesus" or completely "cold to Jesus." The point has nothing to do with spiritual temperature. It has everything to do with the fact that, just like their water supply, the Laodicean Christians made Jesus nauseous because they were useless to him and his kingdom.

Unlike the recipients of the other messages to the churches, the Laodiceans weren't facing any particular hardships, difficulties, trials, or persecution. They enjoyed great prosperity, boasting, "I am rich, I have prospered, and I need nothing" (v 17). The city itself was extremely wealthy. It was a banking center, so they didn't need anyone else's money. When an earthquake destroyed the city in AD 60, they refused financial help from Rome. Instead, they rebuilt the city themselves, and made it even better than it was before, adding gymnasiums and theaters. They were also known for their black wool—they had the latest fashions, produced with the best fabrics. And, if that weren't enough, they had the latest medical technology: eye salve and other ointments to improve health. So the citizens of Laodicea were wealthy, fashionable, and healthy. They were the epitome of prosperity. And so were the *Christians* of Laodicea—Jesus charges the church in Laodicea with looking more like their city than the kingdom of heaven. They were not faithful and true witnesses to the gospel of Christ; they were worldly. Their affluence led them to self-sufficiency, making them complacent in this world and useless to Jesus and his kingdom. So, Jesus declares, *You make me sick!*

The temptations of prosperity continue to plague the church today; it continues to deceive us into self-sufficiency. We grow comfortable in our affluence, and we think we can rely on ourselves to fix our own problems. If we get hungry, we'll buy some food. If we get injured, we've got medical insurance. If we want a holiday, we've got a credit card. If we get old, we've got a pension plan. It's not necessarily wrong to have any of these things—but a godly attitude daily recognizes that everything we have comes from the generous hands of our Creator, not from our hard-earned paycheck.

Is it possible you've grown self-sufficient? One of the greatest evidences of this attitude is a lack of prayer. Why would we need to ask God to give us things when we rely on ourselves to get them? Consider your own prayer life. What does it reveal: dependence on God or independence? Reliance on God or reliance on self? Think about it. Do you consider moving for a new job without praying? Pastor, do you lead your church in much planning and strategizing without serious prayer? Is prayer prominent in our corporate worship gatherings or is it minimal?

Another indicator of our self-sufficiency is our willingness to live the Christian life in isolation from other believers. We willingly move to a new city for a better job, without even considering if there is a good gospel church nearby. If church isn't something we think we really need, we'll gather with God's people only when it's convenient or we have nothing better to do. And when our life falls apart, God forbid we should let any of our Christian brothers or sisters know so they can help us carry our burdens. In these and a thousand other ways, we show our self-sufficiency when we don't run to Jesus or to the graces he's provided us with for our times of need.

As a church, the wealth of resources available to us may tempt us to rely on our own efforts and creativity to reach our community or grow the church. "What we really need is to print some cool flyers… or buy a new curriculum… or provide free food at our next event…" Whereas for pastors and church leaders, the wealth of resources available to us may tempt us to neglect prayerful sermon preparation—who needs to ask for God's Spirit when we've got Logos Bible Software, right?

That's why we need to be reminded continually that the greatest danger facing the church today is NOT government legislation; it's NOT outright religious persecution; it's NOT even false teachers or bad doctrine; it's a prosperity that deceives us into self-sufficiency.

Of course, most of us don't think of ourselves as wealthy. Ask most people how much you need to earn to be classed as rich, and their answer would essentially be, "More than I do!" That's because wealth is relative. And *relative to the rest of the world*, we in the West are very wealthy. We are rich in financial resources. We are rich in material resources. We are rich in human resources. And we must continually fight against the danger of self-sufficiency. We must not allow ourselves to be deceived into thinking that our church is doing well because our members are giving and our budget is great. We must resist the idea that we have God's favor because we have a wealth of talented members, leaders, and workers. We must guard against the false notion that God is blessing us because our gatherings are overflowing with visitors and our membership is increasing. Such prosperity is not necessarily a sign of God's blessing.

The reason prosperity is lethal is because it blinds us to our true spiritual condition. In their own minds, the Laodiceans were rich and needed nothing. But in fact, declares Jesus, they are "wretched, pitiable, poor, blind, and naked" (v 17). They aren't just poor; they are, as we say in the US, dirt poor. In their own minds, they have the medical technology to cure eye disease and improve vision. But Jesus declares that they are blind. Finally, while they may be able to boast about their wool and the latest fashions, they are actually naked.

You see, the problem with feeling self-sufficient is that we are not, in fact, sufficient. And if we haven't recognized this, we haven't really embraced the gospel.

Rely on Jesus, Not Yourself

Instead of relying on their material riches, Jesus counsels the Laodicean Christians "to buy from me gold refined by fire, so that you may be rich" (v 18). Jesus offers them true wealth if they will simply rely on him. Jesus' wealth does not perish or rust; his wealth cannot be stolen or destroyed.

So how do we obtain it? I think Paul, following Jesus' teaching, gives us a clear answer in 1 Timothy 6 v 17: "As for the rich in this present age, charge them not to be haughty, nor to set their hopes on the uncertainty of riches, but on God, who richly provides us with everything to enjoy." Prosperity perverts the object of our hope. Rather than relying on the God who supplies all our needs—and finding the joy and security we crave in our relationship with him—we put our hope in his "stuff": the things he provides. But when we reorient our hope toward God, we are free to be generous and rich in good works, "thus storing up treasure for [ourselves] as a good foundation for the future, so that [we] may take hold of what is truly life" (1 Timothy 6 v 19). Don't trust in the fleeting wealth of this world; rely on Jesus and store up treasures in heaven.

Jesus also counsels the Laodicean church to "buy from me … white garments so that you may clothe yourself and the shame of your nakedness may not be seen." The Laodiceans may have been the most fashionable Christians in Asia Minor in their black wool, but Jesus exposes their "nakedness." Ever since Adam and Eve, nakedness has been associated with shame in Scripture. White garments in Revelation point to righteousness. So Jesus is saying, *Rely on me for your righteousness.* In our own strength and power, we cannot produce the righteous life God requires for entrance into the new creation. But by faith in Christ, we are clothed with the righteousness of Christ and receive the promise of justification, being declared acceptable before the holy God. But we must continue to rely on Christ to grow in the righteousness that gives evidence that we are truly justified. The righteousness God requires is not the basis for our salvation; it is the evidence that we have been saved. And this righteousness is something we grow in as we rely on Christ.

Finally, Jesus counsels the Laodicean Christians to "buy from me … salve to anoint your eyes, so that you may see."

Though they have the latest medical applications to heal their eyes, the Laodicean church is so blinded by their prosperity that they cannot see their need for Christ. Only Jesus can open blind eyes to see spiritual truth. If they will but rely on him, he promises to open their spiritual eyes.

As we assess our own hearts, we must ask: on what or on whom are we relying? Are we relying on Jesus or are we relying on ourselves? Are we placing our hope in Jesus or are we hoping in what Jesus gives us? Are we so deceived that we too are spiritually poor, naked, and blind? Take a moment to assess your heart right now:

- What consumes your daily thoughts? Do you daydream about spending an eternity with Jesus, or extending your life on earth as long as possible with gym memberships and organic foods? Do you think more about obtaining a second vacation home, or entering into God's house for all eternity?

- What dominates your financial budget? Do you seek to be generous with the blessings God has given you, even if it means personal sacrifice, or do you give merely what you have left over, if you even have anything "left over"? Are you living within your financial means in order to free yourself to be generous, or are you overextending yourself financially, just to keep up with your neighbors?

- How about when things aren't going so well? Do you find solace in a tub of ice-cream or a bottle of vodka, or do you run to Christ, who provides what we need? Do you turn to retail therapy to make you feel better, trying to fix your problems by spending money on them, or do you turn to Christ, who offers to give you the water of life at no cost?

- What about your church? Is it only a social club where people are made to feel comfortable in their affluence? Is it a place where people meet up over coffee to chat about their new car and their kids' schools? Or does your church expose the idols of materialism and possessions? Does it encourage living a life informed by the gospel and all its demands?

Jesus calls us, both as individuals and churches, to buy from him spiritual wealth, clothes, and eye-salve. But how do we "buy" spiritual things from Jesus?

We find the answer in Revelation 22 v 17, where Jesus invites all who hear this prophecy and are thirsty to "come" and "take the water of life without price." This language comes from Isaiah 55. There, God asks, "Why do you spend your money for that which is not bread, and your labor for that which does not satisfy? Listen diligently to me, and eat what is good, and delight yourselves in rich food. Incline your ear, and come to me; hear, that your soul may live" (Isaiah 55 v 2-3). To "come, buy and eat ... without money and without price" simply means to rely on God, to come to HIM (Isaiah 55 v 1). And this is precisely what Jesus is saying to the self-sufficient Laodicean Christians. This is exactly what Jesus is saying to all of us self-sufficient Christians—to come to him and rely on him by faith.

Living Zealously

The opposite of self-sufficient complacency is God-reliant zeal. Because the Laodicean Christians have grown self-sufficient and complacent in their prosperity, Jesus commands them to "be zealous and repent" (Revelation 3 v 19). This means reorienting their thinking and leaving their self-sufficiency behind. To do that, they will need to change the way they view wealth—and the same is true for us. One of the keys to overcoming the lure of materialism is generosity. We need to reorient our thinking to understand that the Ruler of creation provides everything we need. And everything he provides above and beyond our needs is meant to be invested in the work of the heavenly kingdom. As we do that, we begin to realize that maybe we "need" much less than we thought we did. We begin to get excited about being the means God uses to provide for others. Can you imagine a church that's zealous in generosity? What might that look like? I think it looks something like the church in Macedonia, who begged "earnestly for the favor of taking part in the relief of the saints" (2 Corinthians 8 v 4). If you want to know what you truly rely on, look at your bank account.

The Laodiceans must also change the way they think about fashion if they're to become spiritually clothed. I have five daughters, and I've never enjoyed clothes shopping. But because I enjoy being with my girls (and having a say in what they wear), I go. Over the many years of traipsing round clothing stores and sitting outside changing rooms, one thing has become clear to me: our culture is consumed by consumerism. We spend (waste) so much money on fashion (if you can call it that) and fill our closets until they're overflowing. I myself have so many clothes that I have given away shirts that I bought on a whim but never wore. But instead of being zealous for earthly fashion, Jesus calls us to be zealous for the heavenly garments of righteousness. Instead of being busy enjoying our wealth, we're to be busy being like Jesus. What if we and our churches were zealous to clothe ourselves in righteousness? What if we were consumed with obeying God's word and keeping Jesus' commandments? What if we were zealous to encourage one another to love and good deeds until Christ returned or we breathed no more?

But why do we find this so difficult? Why is it so hard to see our self-sufficiency, our consumerism, our complacency? Oh that's right, I almost forgot—it's because we're blind. So, we need to change the way we think about sight if we are to receive spiritual vision to see our real needs. The good news is that if we truly belong to Christ, his love for us is such that he will not let us go. If we continue to listen to the counsel of the world rather than the counsel of the risen King, he will "reprove and discipline" those he loves in order to bring them back to himself. This is a kindness of our Lord, though initially his discipline seems painful (Hebrews 12 v 11). So, as soon as Jesus exposes your nakedness in some way, repent. Repent of your self-sufficiency, and come and rely on Jesus alone.

A Money-Can't-Buy Experience

I am continually humbled and convicted by Jesus' tenderness toward sinners. Though the church in Laodicea receives his most severe rebuke, they also receive the greatest promise: that of intimate fellowship at the table of the King. "Behold," says Jesus, "I stand at the door and knock. If anyone hears my voice and opens the door, I will come in to him and eat with him, and he with me" (Revelation 3 v 20). At the moment, Jesus is on the outside—it's a tragic scene. Because of their self-sufficiency, they have virtually locked Jesus outside the church doors. This verse is not an evangelistic appeal. This is Jesus saying, *Though you make me sick, I love you and won't let you go. So, I'm outside your door knocking.* If the Laodicean Christians recognize their self-sufficiency and repent, they will open the door and let Jesus in. To those who come to Jesus and rely on him alone for true wealth, righteousness, and life, Jesus offers a place at his table. This is the greatest promise of all—to dwell in the house of the Lord forever in his presence. Sitting at the dinner table with King Jesus—now that really is a money-can't-buy experience.

But Jesus—the Ruler over all creation (v 14)—also offers us a different kind of seat: "The one who conquers, I will grant him to sit with me on my throne, as I also conquered and sat down with my Father on his throne" (v 21). While on earth, Jesus was "a faithful and true witness," even unto death. He walked the road marked with suffering in order to save us. But the Father vindicated Jesus by raising him from the dead on the third day and exalting Jesus to his right hand. And as we follow Jesus, though he may lead us on the road marked with suffering, we begin to realize that these painful roads are the roads to our resurrection and glory. By faith, we have been united to Jesus in his life, death, resurrection, and exaltation. We've been adopted as royal sons and daughters—and on that final day, instead of being judged, we'll be vindicated before our enemies as we too share in our King's judgment (2 v 26-27; 20 v 4).

You Do It, Jesus

I have the joy of being grandfather to a vivacious and gregarious three-year-old. She's at that age when she has complete and utter confidence in her ability to do everything for herself. She's self-reliant, self-sufficient. One evening as I was walking her and her parents to their car, I opened the car door and began to lift her to her car seat, and she rebuked me, saying, "I do it! I do it!" In a toddler, it was cute and funny. But very quickly I was reminded of the satanic roots of "I do it." It was the same lie Satan got Adam and Eve to believe: *God won't let you do it on your own. YOU do it! YOU do it!* And the lie has not changed. You see, if Satan can get us to believe that we can do it all ourselves, then he's deceived us into thinking we don't need Christ.

But Jesus is the faithful and true witness, who not only tells us the truth about our Father in heaven; he also tells us the truth about our spiritual condition. We cannot hide who we are from him. He truthfully exposes our self-deception and shows us our sin and shame until we're forced to admit: "I can't deal with this myself. YOU do it, Jesus."

It's when we do this that we're freed to enjoy with thanksgiving all the good things that God blesses us with. But they will no longer consume us, because we can hold them with a loose hand. Instead we'll fix our hope on heavenly treasures, and live zealously for Christ's heavenly kingdom.

There's sometimes a mistaken notion that when you become a Christian, Jesus takes away all your troubles and everyone lives happily ever after. Now that you've read about the dangers facing your church, I trust that idea has been dispelled. But even before reading this book, I'm sure that if you embraced Christ expecting a fast-tracked fairytale ending, then you had already been disappointed. Prince Charming still hasn't come; the wicked stepmother still rules; the self-absorbed stepsisters still persecute you; and you're still scrubbing floors.

And yet, the desire for "happily ever after" is hard-wired in us; we still long for it. The problem is that we look for our "happily ever after" to come by the wrong persons, in the wrong places, at the wrong time. The Bible's story is about a faithful, righteous Prince who becomes King, and rescues a filthy, adulterous bride in order to make her beautiful for their wedding day. But the dragon, the King's archenemy, seeks to destroy the King before he can rescue his bride. Nevertheless, the King slays the dragon and after ascending to his throne, he begins preparing his bride for the wedding feast. In the meantime, after failing to destroy the King, the dragon now seeks to destroy the King's bride. He uses every weapon at his disposal: tyrannical government (described in Revelation as "the beast"), corrupt religion ("the false prophet"), sinful humanity ("those who dwell on the earth"), and immoral culture ("the great prostitute").

The language of Revelation reads like a fairytale, except we know that this one's true. Jesus is the King, who is now risen and reigning. Satan is the dragon, now defeated and desperate. And we, the church, are the King's bride under attack. Through his vicious, unrelenting war against us, Satan makes this life a living hell for the church. So long as Satan roams this earth like a lion seeking to devour its prey, the church faces many dangers. Satan doesn't care if we pursue truth to the neglect of love or if we pursue love to the neglect of truth; both extremes undermine the gospel. He uses fear of death as a weapon against us, and he doesn't care if it results in denial of Christ or in doctrinal compromise; they both accomplish the same end. He doesn't care whether we think too much of ourselves or not enough; both are equally detrimental to the mission of the church.

In the face of all these dangers, Revelation dares to speak the question that's on every disappointed Christian's lips: "O Sovereign Lord, holy and true, how long before you will judge and avenge our blood on those who dwell on the earth?" (6 v 10) *How long will this go on for?* Thankfully, as the book of Revelation develops, it also dares to give an answer to our pressing question. While faithful Christians may disagree as to the precise timings of the events in Revelation 4 – 22, we can all agree that Jesus, the risen and reigning King, will return to vindicate us and bring us to God. Here's how the plot will unfold:

- The returning King will defeat the rebellion of sinful humanity once and for all in the final battle (16 v 12-16; 17 v 11-14; 19 v 11-21; 20 v 7-9), and gather the nations for the final judgment (20 v 11-13). All who conquer are promised a share in the returning King's rule and will take part in the final judgment (2 v 26-28; 3 v 21; 20 v 4).

- The returning King will turn the kings of the earth against the immoral city, the "great prostitute," and bring the city to its end (17 v 1-18). All heaven will rejoice (19 v 1-5), and all who conquer will be given white garments (3 v 5; 19 v 8) and will take part in the marriage supper of the Lamb (19 v 6-10).

- The returning King will crush every enemy under his feet, casting Satan, the beast (tyrannical government/ rulers), and the false prophet (false religion/priests) into hell where they will be tormented for all eternity (20 v 10). The last enemy to be destroyed is death, as it too will be cast into the lake of fire (hell), which is the second death (20 v 14). However, all who conquer are promised that they will not taste the second death (2 v 11). Instead, they will be granted to eat from the tree of life in the paradise of God (v 7) and dwell in the presence of God and of the Lamb as priests in God's presence (1 v 6; 5 v 10; 20 v 6).

As we live out our part in God's storyline, Revelation does not shy away from the reality that for the Christian this life is hard and filled with suffering. And it does not blush at the possibility that, in the face of the dangers surrounding us, we will be tempted to give up and give in—to deny Christ or compromise our faith in some way. But Revelation doesn't leave us in despair. Instead, it invites us to view this world from God's perspective of heaven's throne, and shows us the future hope that awaits all who conquer. All who endure to the end by continuing to live with faith in Christ will inherit an eternity with God as his royal sons and daughters, serving as priests in his presence forever. For now, we overcome the dangers facing the church as we look to Christ and long for this future inheritance.

But it's hard to long for a future we can't imagine. That's why Revelation ends by showing us our eternal inheritance in three pictures—pictures meant to capture our imagination and impress eternity upon our memory.

A Beautiful Garden

Every summer my family and I vacation at a beach on the east coast of Florida. I enjoy waking up just before dawn, putting on my exercise gear, and walking on the beach while the sun rises over the ocean. But as glorious as it is, I realize this is but a taste of what God's got in store:

> Then I saw a new heaven and a new earth, for the first heaven and the first earth had passed away, and the sea was no more. (Revelation 21 v 1)

The new heaven and earth will be a renewed and restored creation (see also Isaiah 66 v 17-24). In Revelation, "first" indicates this present age and order. Thus, this "first heaven and the first earth" will pass away. Since "the sea" pictures chaos, evil, and death, these will also come to an end with the passing away of the first heaven and earth, for "the sea [will be] no more."

The description of this new heaven and new earth in Revelation 22 is meant to take our minds back to the description of the Garden of Eden in Genesis 1 and 2. This new Eden will be everything the first was meant to be and more. The river of the water of life (eternal life) will flow from God's throne (Revelation 22 v 1-2); the tree of life will be available to all, even Gentiles (v 2); and the curse of the first Eden will finally be reversed (v 3). God will be there, and all who conquer will have intimate fellowship with him under his ownership, protection, and care. We "will see his face, and his name will be on [our] foreheads" (v 4; 2 v 17; 3 v 12).

When we see the beauty and glory of this present world—the mist on the mountains or the wings of a butterfly or the laughter of loved ones—we should long for the unimaginable beauty and glory of the restored and renewed Eden. Equally, when we see the ugliness and corruption of this present world, we should long for the restored and renewed Eden, where there will be no more sin, death, disease, chaos, and evil. When we see death all around us, we should long to be in the paradise of God, where we may eat freely from the tree of life. And when we feel abandoned, uncared for, and unprotected in this present world, we should long for the renewed and restored Eden, where we will dwell with God in his presence, under his loving care and protection.

A Great City

I love cities. I love the diversity they offer: diversity of food, music, people, architecture. You never know what you're going to find. One cold New Year's Eve, as my wife and I were celebrating our honeymoon in New York City, we came upon a group of people waiting in line at the Cathedral of St. John the Divine. We didn't know why they were waiting, but we got in line anyway. Once inside, we found a seat and quickly realized we were at the Concert for Peace, the first public memorial service for the composer Leonard Bernstein. Since my wife and I are musicians, you can imagine what a joy it was to hear his music performed live. I love that in a large city you can eat at any time of the day or night; you can enjoy jazz or classical music indoors or outdoors; you can enjoy a play on or off Broadway. We're meant to sense something of this excitement and joy in Revelation's description of the "new Jerusalem."

Just as the old earth is passing away, the corrupt city, also known as "Babylon the great" and "the great prostitute" (Revelation 17), gives way to "the holy city, new Jerusalem" (21 v 2). It will be located on God's holy mountain (v 9-21). It will be populated by both Jews and Gentiles, as pictured in the twelve gates representing the tribes of Israel and the twelve foundations representing the apostles of the church (v 12-14). And God will be there in all his glory and radiance (v 11).

But already, all who embrace Christ by faith are citizens of this heavenly city (Galatians 4 v 21-31). And already, we're reminded that this citizenry is diverse, coming "from every tribe and language and people and nation" (Revelation

5 v 9; 7 v 9). The excitement and joy of being part of this city starts now, with our churches. But that creates a tension too—because our citizenship is in heaven, we are sojourners and exiles in this world (1 Peter 2 v 11). We're called to be a holy nation now, distinct from this world in our behavior and calling on all peoples everywhere to repent and embrace King Jesus by faith (v 9).

God's Temple

Finally, our eternal inheritance is pictured as God's temple restored and renewed. In the new heaven and the new earth, God's promise to dwell with his people will be realized in all its fullness (Revelation 21 v 3). God dwelt with his people, Adam and Eve, in the first Eden; God dwelt with his people, Israel, in the Most Holy Place in the tabernacle and temple; and God dwells with his new covenant people in Jesus, the true temple (John 1 v 14). And when Jesus ascended to the Father's right hand, he gave us his Spirit as a down payment of the promise that God would dwell with us (Ephesians 1 v 13-14). In the new heaven and the new earth, we will dwell in God's presence, for, like the Most Holy Place in the temple, the city is a cube and built of precious metals and stones (Revelation 21 v 15-21). Although of course, it's not really fair to say this city is "like" the Old Testament temple. It's the other way around: the earthly temple was a mere imitation of the eternal temple all along.

And yet, in the new creation there is no need for a temple *per se*, for "the Lord God the Almighty and the Lamb" is its temple, and they illuminate the city with their glory (v 22-23). All who conquer—both Jews and Gentiles, kings and peasants, sons and daughters—will enter the city and dwell with God, but "nothing unclean will ever enter it, nor anyone who does what is detestable or false, but only those who are written in the Lamb's book of life" (v 27).

Until Christ returns, we who have received his Spirit are now God's temple—that's the church. That's *your* church (1 Peter 2 v 4-8). This "temple" is being built on the foundation of the gospel given to the New Testament apostles and prophets (Ephesians 2 v 19-22). The church is also a priesthood, with special access to God's presence, serving him and offering our lives as living, spiritual sacrifices before him (1 Peter 2 v 5; Romans 12 v 1).

But all this is just the prologue. The possession of the Spirit as a down payment should cause us to long for the day when we will dwell with God and he with us in unhindered, unmediated fellowship. For it is in God's presence that we will receive all the promises God has made to us in Christ Jesus.

Happy Ever After Is Coming

Church, this life is not our "happily ever after." For now, the church continues to be under satanic attack. For now, the church faces suffering and persecution and death. For now, the church struggles along with distractions and divisions and disappointments.

Your church faces dangers, but don't lose hope—because all who endure faithfully to the end will return to the restored Eden. We will dwell in the most holy and glorious new Jerusalem. And most importantly, we will live in God's presence, where there will be no more pain, no more sorrow, no more cancer, no more birth defects, no more broken marriages, no more sibling rivalries, no more external hostilities, no more oppressive governments, no more evil, no more death. Everyone who conquers "will have this heritage, and [God] will be his God and he will be [God's] son" (Revelation 21 v 7).

Your church faces dangers, but don't try to brush them aside—let them cause you to long for Christ's return. All the sin and evil we now experience remind us that this world is corrupt and needs to be renewed. All the dangers we now face as a church push us to long for the return of Christ, when he will vindicate us and bring us into our eternal home.

Your church faces dangers, but don't ignore them. Instead, let them awaken you from your spiritual slumber and spur you on toward greater zeal for Christ and the mission he has given his church. For too long, we've been asleep. The time to awaken is now.

Your church faces dangers, but don't be paralyzed by fear. Do something about them! Decide which two dangers your church is most at risk of, and then prayerfully consider what needs to change. It is one thing to see the traps; but now we need to step out in faith and trust the guide to navigate around them.

Your church faces dangers, but don't be surprised. Jesus has given us the words of Revelation "to show his servants what must soon take place" in order that we would not be taken aback by the coming difficulties (22 v 6). We can trust these promises because Jesus' words are trustworthy and true (21 v 5), and as the Alpha and the Omega, the beginning and the end, he both initiates history and brings it to its conclusion (21 v 6). Jesus is God's King, sovereign over all history, and he will accomplish all his holy will.

We are not promised "happily ever after" in this life, but rest assured, our "happily ever after" is coming. Our King has already slayed the dragon. He will return for his perfected bride. And he will bring us home.

When? He is coming soon! So, prepare yourself, and pray, "Come, Lord Jesus" (22 v 20)!

Until that day, "the grace of the Lord Jesus be with all. Amen" (v 21).

Chapter 1

The quote on page 31 is from Paul Tripp, *What Did You Expect? Redeeming the Realities of Marriage* (Crossway, 2010), p 188.

Chapter 2

For information on the context in Smyrna see:
* Grant Osborne, "Revelation" in *The Baker Exegetical Commentary on the New Testament* (Baker, 2004), p 128.
* G. K. Beale, *The Book of Revelation: A Commentary on the Greek Text* (Eerdmans, 1999), p 30-31.

For information on the situation in present-day Iraq see:
* Moni Basu, "In biblical lands of Iraq, Christianity in peril after ISIS," CNN.com, online: http://www.cnn.com/2016/11/20/middleeast/iraq-christianity-peril/index.html (accessed July 12, 2017).

To read a fuller account of Helen Roseveare's story see:

- Justin Taylor, "A Woman of Whom the World Was Not Worthy: Helen Roseveare (1925-2016)," online: https://blogs.thegospelcoalition.org/justintaylor/2016/12/07/a-woman-of-whom-the-world-was-not-worthy-helen-roseveare-1925-2016 (accessed September 15, 2017).

The account of Polycarp can be found in:

- M. W. Holmes, *The Apostolic Fathers: Greek texts and English translations*, Updated ed. (Baker Books, 1999), p 235.

Chapter 3

Information on the news stories referenced at the start of this chapter came from the following sources:

- Sarah Kramer, "ABC Citing 'Hate Group' Label as Fact is Not Only False, But Irresponsible," Alliance Defending Freedom, July 14, 2017, online: http://blog.adflegal.org/detailspages/blog-details/allianceedge/2017/07/15/video-abc-citing-hate-group-label-as-fact-is-not-only-false-but-irresponsible (accessed July 15, 2017).
- "Tim Farron's resignation raises questions about the line between public policy and private belief," The Economist, June 16, 2017, online: https://www.economist.com/blogs/erasmus/2017/06/liberals-logic-and-sin (accessed July 14, 2017).
- "US Supreme Court to decide Colorado gay wedding cake case: A timeline of events," Fox News, June 26, 2017, online: http://www.foxnews.com/us/2017/06/26/us-supreme-court-to-decide-colorado-gay-wedding-cake-case-timeline-events.html (accessed July 14, 2017).
- Daniel S. Levine, "Jack Phillips: 5 Fast Facts You Need

to Know," Heavy.com, June 29, 2017, online: http://
heavy.com/news/2017/06/jack-phillips-supreme-
court-colorado-masterpiece-cakeshop-baker-religion/
(accessed July 14, 2017).

- Kelley Moody, "Local teacher says religion may have cost
him his job," KESQ.com, August 29, 2016, online: http://
www.kesq.com/home/local-teacher-says-religion-may-
have-cost-him-his-job/63268489 (accessed, September
17, 2017.

For a brief explanation of the setting in Pergamum, see:

- Grant R. Osborne, "Revelation" in *The Baker Exegetical
Commentary on the New Testament* (Baker, 2002), p 138-40.

Chapter 4

For a fuller explanation of the situation in Thyatira, see:

- Grant R. Osborne, "Revelation" in *The Baker Exegetical
Commentary on the New Testament* (Baker, 2002), p 153.
- B. D. Bratka, "Apollo," in J. D. Barry, D. Bomar, D.
R. Brown, R. Klippenstein, D. Mangum, C. Sinclair
Wolcott, … W. Widder (Eds.), *The Lexham Bible
Dictionary* (Lexham Press, 2016).
- Gary M. Burge, "Thyatira," in D. N. Freedman, A. C.
Myers, & A. B. Beck (Eds.), *Eerdmans Dictionary of the
Bible* (W.B. Eerdmans, 2000), p 1308.
- B. J. Beitzel, "Thyatira," in W. A. Elwell, ed., *The Baker
Encyclopedia of the Bible*, Vol. 2 (Baker Book House,
1988), p 2059.

Chapter 5

For an explanation on the use of numbers symbolically in
Revelation see:

- Grant Osborne, "Revelation" in *The Baker Exegetical Commentary on the New Testament* (Baker, 2004), p 701.
- Sam Storms, *Kingdom Come: The Amillennial Alternative* (Mentor, 2013), p 456.

Don Carson on losing the gospel in one generation:

- Justin Taylor, "It Only Takes One Generation for the Church To Die," The Gospel Coalition, online: https://blogs.thegospelcoalition.org/justintaylor/2011/07/24/it-only-takes-one-generation-for-a-church-to-die/ (accessed July 22, 2017).

Chapter 6

Information on the background in Philadelphia can be found in:

- Grant Osborne, "Revelation" in *The Baker Exegetical Commentary on the New Testament* (Baker, 2004), p 189-90.

For statistics on average church size in the USA see:

- Hartford Institute for Religion Research, "Fast Facts about American Religion," online: http://hirr.hartsem.edu/research/fastfacts/fast_facts.html#numcong (accessed August 1, 2017). The Hartford Institute (USA) estimates that there are about 314,000 "Protestant and other Christian churches in the United States." Of those 314,000 congregations, half have 75 or less persons in attendance on Sunday mornings. Most of the churches in the United States have less than two hundred in attendance on Sunday morning.

To read the full story of Spurgeon's conversion see:

- Justin Taylor, "How the Snowpocalypse of 1850 Led to Spurgeon's Conversion 164 Years Ago Today," The Gospel

Coalition, online: https://blogs.thegospelcoalition.org/justintaylor/2014/01/06/charles-spurgeons-conversion-in-a-primitive-methodist-chapel (accessed July 31, 2017).

Chapter 7

For more on the links between Revelation 2 v 14-22 and Isaiah 65 see:

- J. Alec Motyer, *The Prophecy of Isaiah: An Introduction and Commentary* (IVP, 1993), p 528-28.

MORE FROM JUAN SANCHEZ

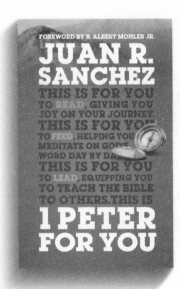

Juan Sanchez brings his experience of ministry in the US and Latin America, and his pastoral wisdom and insight, to this wonderful epistle—an epistle that every Christian needs to treasure today. Part of the *God's Word For You* series of expository guides which walk you through books of the Bible verse by verse.

Christians are nowhere promised that they will escape the struggles and difficulties which are common to all humanity: poverty, disease, broken relationships, and death. The key question that Peter addresses in his first letter is this: how should we respond to the suffering we experience? This guide contains six Bible studies for small groups and individuals.

21 MINISTRY VALUES FOR GROWING CHURCHES

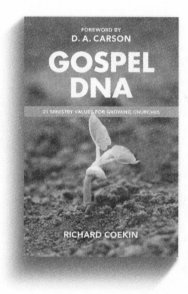

Acts chapter 20 tells how Paul sat down to train the elders of the Ephesian church he had planted some years before. The principles of gospel ministry he lays down are simple, but absolute dynamite.

In 21 simple, practical principles, Richard Coekin sets out how this "Gospel DNA" should shape our approach to building churches today.

This book draws on his experience as director of the London-based Co-Mission church-planting initiative in the UK. It will help you be part of a dynamic strategy for growing gospel churches today.

Includes a foreword by D.A. Carson

thegoodbook.com/dna
thegoodbook.co.uk/dna

thegoodbook
COMPANY

BIBLICAL | RELEVANT | ACCESSIBLE

At The Good Book Company, we are dedicated to helping Christians and local churches grow. We believe that God's growth process always starts with hearing clearly what he has said to us through his timeless word—the Bible.

Ever since we opened our doors in 1991, we have been striving to produce resources that honor God in the way the Bible is used. We have grown to become an international provider of user-friendly resources to the Christian community, with believers of all backgrounds and denominations using our Bible studies, books, evangelistic resources, DVD-based courses, and training events.

We want to equip ordinary Christians to live for Christ day by day, and churches to grow in their knowledge of God, their love for one another, and the effectiveness of their outreach.

Call us for a discussion of your needs or visit one of our local websites for more information on the resources and services we provide.

Your friends at The Good Book Company

NORTH AMERICA		thegoodbook.com		866 244 2165
UK & EUROPE		thegoodbook.co.uk		0333 123 0880
AUSTRALIA		thegoodbook.com.au		(02) 9564 3555
NEW ZEALAND		thegoodbook.co.nz		(+64) 3 343 2463

WWW.CHRISTIANITYEXPLORED.ORG
Our partner site is a great place for those exploring the Christian faith, with a clear explanation of the good news, powerful testimonies and answers to difficult questions.